H E R O E S

———

A N D

———

Z E R O E S

———

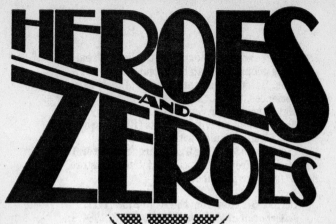

TERRY POWELL

VICTOR BOOKS™

A DIVISION OF SCRIPTURE PRESS PUBLICATIONS INC.
USA CANADA ENGLAND

Heroes and Zeroes explores the lives of real
Bible people who had both triumphs and failures. Based on biblical accounts of their experiences, this book draws out spiritual truths
and principles for young people to live by today. Student activity booklets (Rip-Off Sheets)
and a leader's guide with visual aids
(SonPower Multiuse Transparency Masters) are
available from your local Christian bookstore
or from the publisher.

Scripture taken from the *Holy Bible, New
International Version,* © 1973, 1978, 1984, International Bible Society. Used by permission of Zondervan Bible Publishers. Other
Scripture quotations are from *New Ameri-
can Standard Bible* (NASB), © the Lockman
Foundation 1960, 1962, 1963, 1968, 1971,
1972, 1973, 1975, 1977. Verses marked TLB are
taken from *The Living Bible,* © 1971, Tyn-
dale House Publishers, Wheaton, IL 60189.
Used by permission.

Interior illustrations by Terry Sirrell

Library of Congress Catalog Card Number:
86-63150

ISBN: 0-89693-570-1

Recommended Dewey Decimal
Classification: 248.83

Suggested Subject Heading: YOUTH—
RELIGIOUS LIFE

CONTENTS

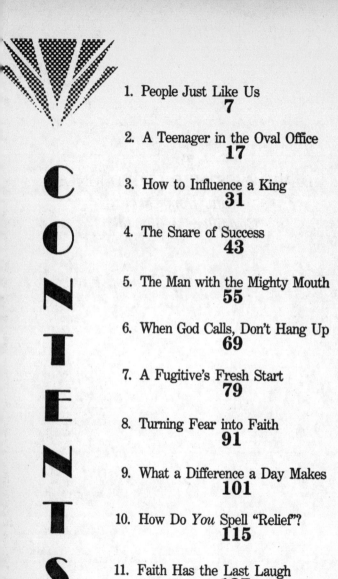

To
DAVID & ESTHER LLOYD-JONES
Gifts from God
Gap-fillers in my life

PEONLE JUST LIKE US

Back in October 1985, millions of us oohed and aahed over a refrigerator. It wasn't the kind mass-produced by Frigidaire, which chills your Dr Pepper. It was a flesh-and-blood model—a player on the defensive line of the Chicago Bears: William "the Refrigerator" Perry.

How did Perry become a household name?

During a nationally televised Monday night football game, the Bears coach inserted the 308-pound behemoth *as a running back!* Twice he blocked for another back, bowling over defensive linemen and clearing a path to the goal line for his teammate. And to everyone's surprise, Perry plowed through for one touchdown of his own.

Reporters pounced on the story. Within days, millions were following Perry's offensive exploits. He scored three other touchdowns that season—one as a pass receiver!

Loyalists organized a fan club. Members received a square "72" refrigerator magnet celebrating Perry's jersey number. Talk show hosts rolled out the red carpet. Advertisers asked him to hawk their products. "The offers are coming in at the rate of 15 an hour," said his agent in midseason. McDonald's, Coca-Cola, and big refrigerator makers like Whirlpool and General Electric were among the companies dialing his number. A manufacturer of thermal underwear that signed Perry to a promotional contract boasted, "We keep the Refrigerator warm." His endorsements raked in more cash than his four-year, $1.35-million football contract.

The rookie's popularity had mushroomed, despite his missing most of training camp in a contract dispute. When he finally reported, he was so overweight that his own defensive coach labeled him a "wasted draft pick." Within weeks, though, after reaching his "trimmed-down" playing weight of 308 pounds, even that coach was lauding the unusual athletic feats of "the Refrigerator." He went on to help the Bears become Super Bowl champions that year.

What happened to Perry illustrates how media hype can help create a celebrity. Public exposure of athletes, actors, musicians, and politicians can swoosh them from obscurity to fame in no time.

Nobody knows how long "the Refrigerator" will be a hot item, but public infatuation with him will eventually wane. Then TV and newspapers will blow the trumpet for somebody else. That's how the "celebrity syndrome" works. Headlines and notoriety are fleeting.

ENDURING HEROES

No one enjoyed swapping William Perry anecdotes more than I did. But I'd like to make a life-transforming recommendation. Balance your affection for contemporary celebrities with an interest in people who have "staying power." Imitate folks who lived a long time ago but whose stories are *still* fresh with meaning. People whose lives stand the test of time deserve our attention even more than media-hatched heroes of the present era. Especially if those stories are recorded in what continues to be the number one bestseller—the Bible.

Personalities in the Bible didn't have the ABC Sports Network, "The Tonight Show," or *People* magazine to spread their fame. Yet God figured that their experiences were worth putting into His Holy Word.

Emerson said, "Those who follow after celebrity sip the foam of many lives." I want to taste more than foam—don't you? When you read about folks in the Bible, you'll find substance, not foam. I can guarantee it because every part of God's Word is inspired and offers practical help for daily living.

Elie Wiesel said, "God made man because He loves stories." This book relates the stories of a few Bible people. In the next 10 chapters, you'll meet all kinds of folks. And you'll understand why their stories have been around for thousands of years.

Before we roll back the curtain on their lives, though, let me share some reasons for making Bible character studies a lifelong pursuit. Sure, I want to lure you into the following chapters. But more than that, I want you to reap the spiritual benefits of ongoing association with people in God's Word.

GOOD GUYS WEAR GRAY HATS
You'll identify with people in the Bible. God's biographical sketches offer realistic portraits that aren't sugarcoated.

Heroes have their problems too.

Oliver Cromwell once laid down the terms on which he would grant a sitting to Lely, the renowned painter. "Mr. Lely, I desire you would use all your skill to paint my picture truly like me, and not flatter me at all; but remark all these roughnesses, pimples, warts, and everything as you see me, otherwise I will never pay a farthing for it."

Similarly, the written portraits of people in Scripture show "warts and all." And that fact increases their value.

We tend to think: "I could never be as trusting as Abraham."

"I could never pray like David."

"Who can take persecution like Paul?"

"Who can witness like Peter?"

"No way can we identify with folks in the Bible. God made them different for special purposes. They had it all together."

But wait. Not even the so-called "good guys" in the Bible were squeaky clean. No siree. They were chip-off-the-old-block people just like us. Our Bible heroes had flaws like these:

More than once Abraham endangered his wife by lying.

David played around with someone else's wife, then knocked off her husband.

Paul called himself the "chief of sinners."

Peter once denied even knowing Jesus.

If we feel that we can't identify with them, then we can't learn from Bible personalities. But when we grasp the fact that they were *like us*—sometimes strong and loyal, sometimes weak and selfish—we open our minds to important truths. Buried in the "I've-heard-that-a-hundred-times-before" stories are messages such as . . .

• God loves people—not because they're good, but

in spite of their badness.

• God uses people to do extraordinary things—not because they're megatalented, but because they recognize their limitations and lean on His power.

If Bible heroes and heroines were self-sufficient supersaints, they couldn't model for us the need for faith in God. Our identification with their humanity enables us to see God in their lives.

In old TV westerns, you could easily tell the good guys from the bad guys. The good guys wore white cowboy hats. They could go years without spilling ketchup on their shirts or missing a target with their six-guns. The bad guys donned black hats. They spit at anyone who asked them the time of day. In real life, though, the distinction between "good" and "bad" people isn't so clear-cut.

Look closely and you'll see *gray* hats on the heads of even the best known Bible characters. They were "as completely human as we are" (James 5:17, TLB). Come to think of it, I saw a lot of gray hats on folks at church last Sunday too.

LIVING PROOF

Human biographers tend to elevate the positive traits and accomplishments of their subjects. They may unintentionally emphasize appealing features and cover up rough edges. But as I've already pointed out, God's biographical sketches tell it the way it was. He exposes both the righteous and the devilish side of heroes and heroines whom we've heard about since we were knee-high to a gnat.

Such realism reflects the credibility of God's Word. In *You and Your Network* (Word), Fred Smith echoes this point: "One of the proofs of the inspiration of Scripture is that the Bible says things about its

characters that people would not write" (p. 74).
Study Bible people, and your appreciation for the
reliability of God's Word will grow.

TRUTH WITH SKIN ON

Most of us agree that doctrinal statements
and commands couched in the Bible are important.
Yet true statements about God's nature, sin and its
consequences, etc., often come across as academic
and impractical. Similarly, lists of rules governing
human relationships may seem ivory-towerish or ide-
alistic. We may memorize them, but they don't easily
seep into our bloodstreams.

If you aren't too impressed by theory or you wres-
tle with biblical commands that seem sterile, then
make studies of real Bible people a staple item in
your spiritual diet. The slice-of-life anecdotes will
illustrate the reliability of broad statements of truth
and commands found elsewhere in Scripture.

It's one thing to read this truth: "Do not be deceived, God is not mocked; for whatever a man sows,
this he will also reap. For the one who sows to his
own flesh shall from the flesh reap corruption, but
one who sows to the Spirit shall from the Spirit reap
eternal life" (Galatians 6:7-8, NASB). But even more
compelling is the story of a man like Samson, whose
runaway passions resulted in blindness, imprison-
ment, and death in the prime of life. His life gives
deeper meaning to Paul's warning to the Galatians.

I'm grateful for 1 John 1:9: "If we confess our sins,
He is faithful and just and will forgive us our sins and
purify us from all unrighteousness." On the other
hand, seeing how God forgave and used the Apostle
Paul *after* he had been an archenemy of Christianity
encourages me even more. The plot of Paul's life

gives bone, muscle, and breath to the words in 1 John 1:9.

Put simply, Bible people put legs on Bible truths. That's the point Paul was making when he referred the Corinthians to Old Testament accounts of the nation Israel. He cited incidents from their history and said, "Now these things happened as examples for *us.* . . . They were written for *our* instruction" (1 Corinthians 10:6, 11, NASB, italics added).

HELPFUL HEROES
Who are your heroes?

How you answer that question says a lot about you. Dr. J.C. Cain of the Mayo Clinic, when selecting the young medical men to be trained there, had difficulty because of the exceptionally high caliber of the applicants. All had excellent grades, high motivation, and sound work habits. Dr. Cain wrestled with some way to differentiate between them. He decided to ask each prospect this question: "Young man, who are your heroes?" The doctor discovered that this was the best clue to their value structure, and one indicator of their future potential. (Gleaned from *You and Your Network,* p. 69.)

As suggested at the beginning of this chapter, modern society is swamped with celebrities. We idolize individuals with magazine-cover looks or extraordinary talents. But there's a difference between fame or ability, and heroism. Folks who deserve the label "hero" or "heroine" have character qualities or attitudes worth imitating. Old-fashioned traits like unselfishness, persistence, or the capacity to overcome obstacles catapult them to prominence or significance. Celebrities may dazzle us, but heroes enlarge us.

Bible history teems with people who deserve our admiration, whose lives inspire us to reach our God-given potential. We've already emphasized how imperfect they were. But snapshots that show their mistakes don't minimize their positive characteristics and feats. In God's eyes, a model or hero isn't a self-sufficient person. Rather, he's someone who illustrates that dependence on the Lord *is* the basis for growth and accomplishment. Learning from great men and women of the Bible can lift us to greater spiritual heights. Someone put it this way: "Those who want to be eagles can't spend all their time with turkeys."

Not all the characters you'll meet in this book deserve the "hero" name tag. You'll meet a couple whose attitudes and actions you definitely want to avoid. In those instances, you'll discover what kept them from developing the heroic potential that God implants inside every human being.

When you finish *Heroes and Zeroes*, get a copy of another SonPower book on Bible people, *Nobody's Perfect*. Also check out Lorraine Peterson's *Real Characters in the Making* (Bethany). Her teen-oriented devotional book looks at the ups and downs of 13 men and women of the Old Testament.

In your investigation of Bible characters, you won't find 308-pound running backs, Olympic gymnasts who scored a perfect "10," or Top 40 recording artists. But if you look hard, you might find the Lord. "For whatever was written in earlier times was written for our instruction, that through perseverance and the encouragement of the Scriptures we might have hope" (Romans 15:4, NASB).

In chapter 2, you'll meet a teenager who literally altered the course of an entire nation. How did he do it? Turn the page and find out.

A TEENAGER IN THE
OVAL OFFICE

2 Kings 22:1–23:30; 2 Chronicles 34–35

Some folks have a sense of humor that won't quit—
not even after they die. Recently I came across a few
epitaphs that had been reproduced in a Ripley's Believe It or Not museum. The following remarks are
actually inscribed on gravestones of real people (who,
by the way, probably died laughing).
From Ruidosa, New Jersey:

> HERE LIES JOHN YEAST.
> PARDON ME FOR NOT RISING.

Or what about this one, found in Uniontown,
Pennsylvania:

> HERE LIES JONATHAN BLAKE.
> STEPPED ON THE GAS
> INSTEAD OF THE BRAKE.

Scoot up the map to Middlesburg, Vermont and read
the one undoubtedly conjured up by a henpecked
husband:

> I PUT MY WIFE
> BENEATH THIS STONE
> FOR HER REPOSE—
> AND FOR MY OWN.

Or visit Moultrie, Georgia and read about a man who wanted to make sure someone carried on the family name:

> HERE LIES THE FATHER OF 29.
> HE WOULD'VE HAD MORE,
> BUT RAN OUT OF TIME.

My favorite, though, is etched beneath the name "Solomon Peas." It reads:

> PEAS IS NOT HERE—
> ONLY THE POD.
> PEAS SHELLED OUT
> AND WENT HOME TO GOD.

As I chuckle over those lighthearted inscriptions, I'm reminded that a person's epitaph isn't always chiseled on a gravestone. The word "epitaph" refers to any statement which summarizes, or offers a final judgment on, the life of the deceased. I'm also transported to a more somber state of mind. I mull over how I'd want my gravestone to read, what I'd want others to think and say about me when I'm gone. Unless I miss my guess, you also want an epitaph that reflects a life wisely spent.

That reminds me of the most glowing epitaph I've ever come across in the Bible. It's tucked away in a seldom read narrative portion of the Old Testament. The words describe a little-known king who spearheaded a religious revival among the Jewish people.

With that backdrop, the epitaph speaks for itself:

> Neither before nor after Josiah was there
> a king like him who turned to the Lord as
> he did—with all his heart and with all his
> soul and with all his strength.
> *2 Kings 23:25*

What a tribute! It didn't make Ripley's museum, but it's the kind of epitaph I'd like written about me.

Let's find out more about Josiah. How did he earn such an accolade? What did he do that literally changed a nation? What can we learn from him that can increase the impact of *our* lives?

You'll be interested in the answers to these questions because Josiah performed his most courageous acts while still in his teens!

HAPLESS HERITAGE

Imagine you have been transported back to Judah (the southern region of modern Israel) during the seventh century before Christ. You pick up a copy of the *Jerusalem Herald*, and suddenly you feel right at home. Headlines reflect a troubled world of political intrigue, assassinations, declining sexual morality, and religious confusion. You're in a land populated by God's chosen people, the Jews. Yet the newspaper doesn't mirror the kind of moral atmosphere that you'd expect. The nation is on a spiritual "downer."

That's the environment into which Josiah was born. Let's take a closer look at the snapshot of his times offered in 2 Kings and 2 Chronicles.

First, we see how Josiah's father, Amon, and grandfather, Manasseh, led the people down the

tubes. Take a peek at Manasseh flouting the laws of
God and encouraging the worship of false gods such
as Baal and Asherah:

> He did evil in the eyes of the Lord, follow-
> ing the detestable practices of the nations
> the Lord had driven out before the Israel-
> ites. He . . . erected altars to Baal and
> made an Asherah pole. . . . He bowed
> down to all the starry hosts and wor-
> shiped them. . . . He sacrificed his own
> son in the fire, practiced sorcery and divi-
> nation, and consulted mediums and
> spiritists.
>
> *2 Kings 21:2-3, 6*

Now glance at verse 9: "The people did not listen
[to God's Word]. Manasseh led them astray, so that
they did more evil than the nations the Lord had
destroyed before the Israelites."

Next, try to digest verse 16: "Manasseh also shed
so much innocent blood that he filled Jerusalem from
end to end—besides the sin that he had caused Judah
to commit, so that they did evil in the eyes of the
Lord."

LIKE FATHER, LIKE SON

Now shift to the snapshot of Josiah's father,
Amon, who took after Manasseh:

> Amon was twenty-two years old when he
> became king. . . . He did evil in the eyes
> of the Lord, as his father Manasseh had
> done. He walked in all the ways of his
> father; he worshiped the idols his father

had worshiped, and bowed down to them.
He forsook the Lord, the God of his fa-
thers, and did not walk in the way of the
Lord.

                    2 Kings 21:19-22

Amon reigned only two years, though. Some of his
own officials who were jealous of his seat in Judah's
Oval Office "conspired against him and assassinated
the king in his palace" (v. 23). What happened next?
"Then the people of the land killed all who had plot-
ted against King Amon, and they made Josiah his son
king in his place" (v. 24).

They probably had to jerk Josiah out of a third-
grade math class and whisk him away to take the
oath of office. When they crowned him king, he was
only eight years old!

TIMELY TURNAROUND

When Josiah's dad and granddad died, they
were so crooked that undertakers had to screw them
into the ground! But Josiah wasn't cut from the same
cloth. Throughout a 31-year reign, "he did what was
right in the eyes of the Lord . . . not turning aside to
the right or to the left" (2 Chronicles 34:2).

The turning point of his life came when he was 16
years old: "In the eighth year of his reign, while he
was still young, he began to seek the God of his
father David" (34:3). King David was his great-great-
great- (several times) grandfather. Josiah picked David as his model, and shed the harmful layers of
influence spun around him by Amon and Manasseh.

Because of that decision, the course of a whole
nation was shifted. For four years Josiah mulled over
the implications of his spiritual commitment. Then at

age 20 he began issuing head-turning executive orders:

> He began to purge Judah and Jerusalem of high places, Asherah poles, carved idols and cast images. Under his direction the altars of the Baals were torn down; he cut to pieces the incense altars that were above them, and smashed the Asherah poles, the idols and the images.
> *2 Chronicles 34:3-4*

Six years later, another event altered the orbit of Josiah's reign. While some of his officials were supervising a repair job in the temple, Hilkiah the high priest found a long-lost copy of the Law of the Lord that had been written by Moses, probably the first five books of our Old Testament (34:14). That copy of the ancient scrolls was an eye-popping find. Remember Manasseh? He had dumped the inspired Scriptures and shifted everybody's attention away from God. For decades, no one in the land—not even Josiah—had access to these books, which clearly spelled out the ethical lifestyle and worship practices God expected.

A scribe named Shaphan laced up his running shoes and raced back to the Oval Office. He read the scrolls aloud to Josiah. Despite the reforms he had previously initiated, Josiah was crushed by the contrast he saw between God's standards and the spiritual condition of the country. When he heard the words of the Law, he tore his clothes and wept. Like a scalpel, God's Word cut deeply into his conscience.

Josiah didn't keep God's truth to himself either. He blew the dust off the scrolls and wielded his executive power to make sure that all the inhabitants of

Judah were exposed to the Law. Josiah called a public assembly to make a fresh dedication of his life to God:

> Then the king called together all the elders of Judah and Jerusalem. He went up to the temple of the Lord with the men of Judah, the people of Jerusalem, the priests and the Levites—all the people from the least to the greatest. He read in their hearing all the words of the Book of the Covenant, which had been found in the temple of the Lord. The king stood by his pillar and renewed the covenant in the presence of the Lord—to follow the Lord and keep His commands, regulations and decrees with all his heart and all his soul, and to obey the words of the covenant written in this book.
>
> *2 Chronicles 34:29-31*

God's Word began seeping into the behavior of the people too. For decades, religious feasts such as the Passover had been neglected. But under Josiah, these ceremonies were put back on the calendar.

At age 39, in a skirmish with troops from Egypt, Josiah was killed by an archer. Yet he accomplished more in a relatively short life span than most folks do who live to be 100.

Now that we've sketched his life, let's zoom in on a few characteristics of the man. What made him a hero with substance, rather than a hollow celebrity? What traits in Josiah does the Lord want to blend into *our* character portraits?

COSTLY COMMITMENT

The hinge on which Josiah's life turned was a private decision at age 16. You've already read about how "he began to seek the God of his father David" (2 Chronicles 34:3). The word translated "seek" is a strong one. It means "to beat a path after something; to pursue."

What's amazing about this decision is the context in which he made it. Remember—neither his dad nor granddad ever gathered the clan around the fireplace for family devotions. Neither was he encouraged spiritually by the general population. The majority had jumped on Manasseh and Amon's bandwagon and forgotten about God. Plus it was downright risky to rock the boat and go against the grain of popular opinion. Hadn't his father been assassinated by members of his own cabinet?

Put simply, his decision required courage. But he knew it was more important to be right than to be popular. He chose to take God seriously, at all costs.

Can you identify? Ever feel the pull of the multitudes to shuck God's value system and adopt theirs? Then do what Josiah did. Stop playing around with God. Climb off the fence of indecision and dare to be different.

That may mean you'll respond to God's wooing and finally accept Jesus Christ as your Saviour. If you're already a Christian, it means you'll make a conscious, gut-ripping choice to honor God in every sphere of life—even if it means standing out from the herd around you like a neon sign.

Josiah wasn't afraid to be labeled a fanatic. He knew that in order to make his life count, he could no longer keep God at a comfortable distance. He wasn't like a lot of wishy-washy believers today, who want just enough of God to guarantee escape from eternal flames, but not enough to start remodeling their lifestyles.

When I think of this business of total commitment to God, I'm reminded of these satirical words from Wilbur Rees:

> I would like to buy $3 worth of God, please, not enough to explode my soul or disturb my sleep, but just enough to equal a cup of warm milk or a snooze in the sunshine. I don't want enough of Him to make me love a black man or pick beets with a migrant. I want ecstasy, not transformation; I want the warmth of the womb, not a new birth. I want a pound of the Eternal in a paper sack. I would like to buy $3 worth of God, please. (Quoted in *When I Relax I Feel Guilty* by Tim Hansel, David C. Cook, p. 49)

How unlike Josiah! He invested everything—not mere pocket change. And for 23 years thereafter, God honored that decision. His life echoes the truth of Hebrews 11:6: God "rewards those who earnestly seek Him."

Centuries later, God is still on a safari looking for rare species like Josiah. Cement the following words into your mind: "The Lord looks down from heaven on the sons of men to see if there are any who understand, any who seek God" (Psalm 14:2).

STICK-TO-ITIVENESS

Have you ever put up a basketball hoop and backboard, or watched construction workers pour a sidewalk in a new housing development? Such projects require just the right blend of cement mix and water. Pour it into place, and within hours the mushy mixture sets. What you could stir with a stick one day is firm enough to trample on the next.

That reminds me of a verb we ought to be more familiar with: *to endure.* It means "to harden; to become permanently fixed; to continue in the same state for a long period of time." In a nutshell, something that endures—like concrete—doesn't easily shift, change position, or give in to outside influences. It can take the beating of time and the weight of heavy circumstances. It's dependable over the long haul.

Endurance. Make no mistake about it: that's what set Josiah apart from his contemporaries. He stuck like Superglue to the decision he made at age 16 to follow the Lord. Throughout a 31-year reign, he "did what was right in the eyes of the Lord . . . *not turning aside to the right or to the left*" (2 Chronicles 34:2, italics added).

Josiah's faith was rooted not in convenience, but in conviction. It grew in soil composed not by temporary emotional experiences, but by daily disciplines such as prayer. He didn't flit from one spiritual guru to another; rather, he clung to the Lord with bulldog tenacity. His life provides a case study of Hebrews 12:1: "Let us throw off everything that hinders and the sin that so easily entangles, and let us run with perseverance the race marked out for us."

Christianity is a marathon—not a 100-yard dash. We've all known individuals who burst from the starting blocks with lots of fanfare, but who pulled out of the race halfway through. They publicly professed Jesus for a while, but before long old behavior patterns disqualified them and compromised their testimonies. Put simply, their commitments never hardened. Only God knows if such persons were ever truly converted. In many cases, though, I suspect that "faith that falters before the finish was fickle from the first."

My friend, make a rock-ribbed resolution to imitate Josiah's consistency. Don't believe those who say that you can't avoid a period of rebellion. Don't listen when they whisper, "Even Christians need to 'sow a few wild oats.' Might as well get it out of your system now." What they forget to tell you is that even wild oats have to be harvested later on.

SOFTHEARTED

The Old Testament scrolls which the scribe read aloud to Josiah contained stern warnings to the ancient Jews. God promised to discipline them as a nation if they strayed from His commands. When the country began its spiritual descent, many years before Josiah's time, God sent prophets to nudge the people back to God—but to no avail. They spurned the prophets' warnings just as they had rejected the Law of Moses.

We've seen how Josiah bucked the godless trend and worked for spiritual reform. Yet it was still too late to avoid the consequences of sin previously promised by the scrolls and the prophets. God had to keep His word. He knew that the only long-term solution to their idolatry was severe adversity. That's why He appointed a foreign country—Babylonia—to ransack Judah and hold the entire population hostage for 70 years.

That historical backdrop helps us understand Josiah's reaction when he heard the Old Testament books. He grasped the inevitable: Judah had wandered too far in sin to avoid God's discipline. The stabbing realization caused him to tear his clothes and weep.

His emotional response to God's Word revealed *a tender heart*—a heart sensitive to sin and the devastating consequences it has on people. God yearns for individuals whose hearts are soft enough to be penetrated by His Word. Here's how God reacted to Josiah's display of tenderheartedness:

> Because your heart was responsive and you humbled yourself before God when you heard what He spoke against this place and its people, and because you humbled yourself before Me and tore your robes and wept in My presence, I have heard you, declares the Lord. Now I will gather you to your fathers, and you will be buried in peace. Your eyes will not see all the disaster I am going to bring on this place and on those who live here.
> *2 Chronicles 34:27-28*

Simply translated, God delayed the Babylonian invasion until after Josiah's death. One man's tender heart resulted in a few extra years of stability for a nation.

In an article about Josiah titled "The Teenager Who Made a Difference," Chuck Swindoll confronts us eyeball-to-eyeball with these words:

> I want to ask you to think a lot about a tender heart. Young men, that is one of the most masculine qualities you can offer this world—a heart tender toward God; it isn't at all feminine for a man to be tender toward God. And young woman, it is one

of the most beautiful expressions of a godly life—to be tender toward His Word.

Kids, when are you going to get serious about God? I mean, stop playing "church," stop bad-mouthing your folks, stop giving up "religion," and start getting tough on yourself regarding this Book?

When are you going to allow God to soften your spirit and cultivate within you a tender heart? Not until you do will you have a life like Josiah's. But when you do, believe me, you could change our nation. Yes, *you* . . . you really could. ("Insights," *Insight for Living*, 1984)

Now that you've put Josiah's portrait under the magnifying glass, flip to chapter 3. Read about the influences on his life which fueled complete commitment, cultivated consistency, and formed a tender heart.

HOW TO INFLUENCE
A KING

2 Kings 22:1–23:30; 2 Chronicles 34–35

In a penetrating book titled *Growing Strong in the
Seasons of Life,* pastor Chuck Swindoll relates
an anecdote about a former pro football coach
considered one of the greatest motivators of his
era:

> The late football strategist, Vince
> Lombardi, was a fanatic about fundamen-
> tals. Those who played under his leader-
> ship often spoke of his intensity, his drive,
> his endless enthusiasm for the guts of the
> game. Time and again he would come
> back to the basic techniques of blocking
> and tackling. On one occasion his team,
> the Green Bay Packers, lost to an inferior
> squad. It was bad enough to lose . . . but
> to lose to *that* team was absolutely inex-
> cusable. Coach Lombardi called a practice
> the very next morning. The men sat si-
> lently, looking more like whipped puppies
> than a team of champions. They had no

idea what to expect from the man they feared the most.

Gritting his teeth and staring holes through one athlete after another, Lombardi began: "OK, we go back to the basics this morning. . . . "

Holding a football high enough for all to see, he continued to yell: " . . . gentlemen, *this* is a *football!*" (Multnomah Press, p. 373)

That "back-to-the basics" pep talk chiseled its point into the minds of his players. The Packers went on to claim another championship trophy that year. Chances are, the players didn't want to face Lombardi again the day after a loss!

King Josiah—whom you read about in chapter 2—didn't know much about blocking techniques or quarterback option plays. But he exerted a Lombardi-like influence over the nation of Judah.

Spiritually speaking, God's chosen people had been on the losing end of the score for decades. Idolatry and immorality had infiltrated the team. Then God appointed Josiah to manage this bunch of spiritual underachievers. At age 16, Josiah made a firm commitment to the Lord. Then he put the people through the rigors of correcting their slothful playing habits. He abolished idolatry. When a copy of the original game plan (Mosaic Law) was found, Josiah called a team meeting in Jerusalem. In effect, he told them, "It's time to go back to the basics!" He read aloud from the Law and encouraged wholesale allegiance to it. Under Josiah's leadership, their won-loss record did a flip-flop.

We've already explored Josiah's heroic qualities. He decided to seek the Lord rather than win a popularity contest. He was consistent—never veering from his original spiritual decision. And he was tenderhearted before the Lord.

Now let's shift the focus a bit. What accounted for Josiah's positive spiritual bent? What molded his character and spurred him to achieve for God? A closer look reveals at least two significant influences.

MAGNIFICENT MOM

Crack open your Bible to 2 Kings 22:1 and you'll find these words: "Josiah was eight years old when he became king, and he reigned in Jerusalem thirty-one years. *His mother's name was Jedidah*" (italics added).

Did you notice the almost casual reference to the first major influence on Josiah's life? *He had a godly mother!* The verse doesn't exactly say that she followed the Lord, but we can wrench this conclusion out of the statement.

Her name, Jedidah, meant "beloved of God." If you have observed Old Testament genealogical lists very closely, you know that it's unusual to include the name of the mother. Such lists are more apt to include only the name of the father.

By including Josiah's mom in this narrative, I believe that the Lord is making a subtle statement about her role in his spiritual formation. Remember how godless his dad and granddad had been? Their negative example was apparently offset by the positive influence of his mother. How else can we explain Josiah's sensitivity to God during his early years?

It's easy to take mothers for granted. While I was relaxing with the evening paper recently, the following headline grabbed my attention: "Striking Mother and Her Teenagers Near Agreement." The

UPI story told of a working mom who went on strike against her three teenagers when they complained about housework left undone.

The mom worked as a waitress and part-time school bus driver. Yet the teens still expected her to do all the household chores. When one of them muttered, "Mom, you never do anything!" she officially launched her strike. She stopped cooking meals, washing clothes, vacuuming, and performing other mundane chores. As you can imagine, the mess piled up for the next week or two. She wrote work contracts for the children to sign and had these agreements notarized.

During week two of the strike, the teens gave in and cleaned up the house. But they still refused to sign the contracts. The mother compromised and began making their school lunches again. At the time the article was printed, both sides were hammering out compromises to the contracts. The mom told a reporter, "In the future, work around here will be split up real evenly on a rotating basis. I feel it was a learning experience for the kids and myself. I guess I had been a hindrance to them during growing up years by doing everything for them. And it showed them that they took for granted a lot of what I do as mother."

A GODLY WOMAN'S INFLUENCE

Insensitivity to mothers' contributions isn't limited to the realm of household duties. We also tend to forget about the spiritual impact they can have. Scripture introduces us to many mothers who exerted a powerful influence on their kids.

Hannah was such a woman of God. After many years of marriage, she was still childless. She pleaded her case before the Lord:

> In bitterness of soul Hannah wept much and prayed to the Lord. And she made a vow, saying, "O Lord Almighty, if You will only look upon Your servant's misery and remember me, and not forget Your servant but give her a son, then I will give him to the Lord for all the days of his life."
>
> *1 Samuel 1:10-11*

The Lord answered her request, and she conceived Samuel. She gave the child to Eli the priest so he could better prepare for a life of service to God. But Samuel never outgrew his godly mother's influence.

Or consider Jochebed, Moses' mom. This Jewish mother nurtured Moses only until he reached the age of adoption. Then she had to turn him over to the daughter of the Egyptian ruler, Pharaoh (Exodus 2). Despite living his first 40 years in the palace of a pagan ruler, Moses didn't depart from the early teaching of his mother.

Eunice, mother of Timothy, is another example. After Timothy accepted his first pastorate, the Apostle Paul told him, "Continue in what you have learned and have become convinced of, because you know those from whom you learned it, and how *from infancy* you have known the holy Scriptures, which are able to make you wise for salvation through faith in Christ Jesus" (2 Timothy 3:14-15, italics added). Timothy's mother marked his life with a godly heritage from the day he was born.

Like Josiah, Abraham Lincoln occupied an oval office. Josiah would have seconded this comment by

Lincoln: "No person is poor who has had a godly mother."

Now let's shine the spotlight on *your* home. Do *you* have a godly mother? Or are you twice blessed, having *two* Christian parents? If so, you're richer than you think!

When was the last time you told your folks how much you appreciate the prayers they've said on your behalf? The times they provided taxi service to church youth meetings (before you could drive)? The summer camp experiences they financed?

Well . . . what are you waiting for?

OPEN BIBLE

The second major influence on Josiah was *the Word of God.* A few years before the long-lost Books of the Law were uncovered in the temple, Josiah made a spiritual commitment. Yet when he was exposed to God's Word, that commitment found new avenues of expression.

He didn't shrug his shoulders in apathy. Nor did he just nod in agreement with the words, and then stuff them away in his mental filing cabinet for future reference. No siree! The inspired words he heard broke through his defenses and struck his heart.

He wept over sins exposed by the Law. He shared the Scriptures with the entire nation. And he put the words into practice by reinstating religious ceremonies that the people had neglected. God's Word hit him with volcanic force. He was never the same again.

Perhaps the one thing we take for granted more than our parents is the availability of God's Word. We can get a Bible in any size print and almost any color we want. We can choose a paperback, or opt for

Clarence Clutterton's version of
Bible Search.

the more expensive 20-pound coffee-table edition. We can select a paraphrase that reads like the daily newspaper, or pick up one of the numerous scholarly translations nestled on the bookstore shelf. Add to that the opportunities to hear it taught in Sunday School and worship services, and we see what a choice privilege we have.

Ironically, though, repeated exposure and widespread availability make us forget how priceless the Bible is. There are still around 3,000 languages that do not have a single printed copy of God's Word. And in some Iron Curtain countries, government restrictions prevent private ownership of a Bible. One Bible smuggler said, "I've been to places where most of the pastors have never *seen* a copy of the whole Bible. I went through one village and there were folks who asked me if I would tear out a page of my Bible and just leave a page" (Charles Swindoll, "A Teenager Who Made a Difference," *Insight for Living*, 1984).

ACT ON IT

Overexposure also tends to harden our hearts—unless we prayerfully and consciously try to work out the truth of Scripture in our lives. What follows is the story of a young man who was regularly exposed to God's Word, yet without any long-term change. It's from an article titled "Knowing Isn't Enough," which I wrote for *FreeWay:*

Randy, 25, will never hear his four-year-old boy ask for the car keys. He won't see his baby daughter's first boyfriend. After the divorce a year ago, his former wife remarried and moved out of state with the children.

She couldn't feed the kids because he gambled away most payroll checks in the pool hall. After years of constant bickering and threats of separation, she severed the marriage cord.

Randy has drifted from one job to another. Drunk driving has caused two auto accidents. Disgruntled creditors harass him over unpaid bills.

Unfortunately, Randy's story is not uncommon. But if you had known him as a 17-year-old, you would not have anticipated these negative developments. He earned better-than-average grades. His high school faculty voted him one of the "most likely to succeed" seniors. And, beginning in junior high, he attended every Sunday morning church service for six consecutive years!

His youth group often competed with other church groups in Bible drills. (A leader would announce a reference from the Bible, and the participant who first located and read the verse aloud won a point for his team.) Few could match Randy's quickness during a drill! His participation in Bible studies also revealed a broad grasp of Bible knowledge.

Yet, though this knowledge permeated his mind, it never reached his heart. What he knew about God didn't permanently change him. After leaving his home and church environment, Randy shucked his Christian values and lifestyle. ("Knowing Isn't Enough," *FreeWay*, March 28, 1982)

Exposure to the Bible, though essential for healthy spiritual development, doesn't *automatically* change our lives. God's goal for us when we hear or read His Word is *transformation*, not mere information. Bible content isn't an end in itself. Rather, it's a means of experiencing greater intimacy with the Lord and discovering how our faith should express itself in daily life. James put it this way:

> Do not merely listen to the word, and so deceive yourselves. Do what it says. Anyone who listens to the word but does not do what it says is like a man who looks at his face in a mirror and, after looking at himself, goes away and immediately forgets what he looks like. But the man who looks intently into the perfect law that gives freedom, and continues to do this, not forgetting what he has heard, but doing it—he will be blessed in what he does.
>
> *James 1:22-25*

Josiah understood that the *best* Bible translation is done when we translate it into daily experience. How can we do that? By taking a couple minutes before leaving for church meetings and asking God to reveal some practical applications during the teaching times. By offering a similar prayer before any private reading of Scripture.

Such a discipline acknowledges the Holy Spirit's role in making the Bible come alive for you. You'll be following in David's footsteps. When he read Scripture, he wanted to see more than mere words. That's why he prayed, "Open my eyes that I may see wonderful things in Your law" (Psalm 119:18).

PROBING THE WORD

As you read the Bible, it's also helpful to ask a few questions that can sensitize you to the relevant insights of a passage. Here's a list of questions that I often use. You won't find an answer to every question in every separate passage that you read. But a few of the questions will always point you to some practical insights. This study method is based on the "you're-more-apt-to-find-something-if-you're-looking-for-it" principle.

● How does this Bible passage increase my appreciation for Jesus Christ?

● What reasons for praising God are suggested here?

● What can I learn from the people mentioned here—from their positive or negative examples?

● What truth or principle from these verses encourages me? Why?

● What promises does the passage offer? Do any of the promises have special meaning for me right now?

● What words, phrases, or ideas are *repeated* in this portion of Scripture? What is significant about this repetition?

● What sin or shortcoming does this passage expose in my life?

● How should what I'm reading affect my prayer life?

Approaching God's Word in this way can help create in you the kind of tender heart Josiah had. Whether your mom and dad are positive spiritual influences may be out of your control. But whether you have an open or a closed Bible *is* within your control. (For more details on how to sink your teeth into God's Word, get Terry Hall's SonPower book, *Off the Shelf and into Yourself.*)

This closer look at Josiah's portrait has introduced us to an inescapable principle: *Before we can influence our world, we must submit to divine influences.* Before we can be change agents for the Lord, we've got to let Him change us.

Remember the sidesplitting epitaphs back at the start of chapter 2? There's one other epitaph I didn't mention, and it's the last one I'd want put on *my* gravestone. As you read it, mull over what God's Spirit is nudging you to do in response to this chapter:

HERE LIES A MAN WHO WAS ALWAYS GOING TO...

NOW HE'S GONE.

THE SNARE OF SUCCESS
2 Chronicles 26:1-23

Have you ever witnessed the execution of a frog? Lots of teens have—in a high school chemistry class. The teacher puts the unsuspecting creature in a large beaker of cool water. Then he scoots a Bunsen burner beneath the beaker and ignites a very low flame. That small flame heats the water very slowly— several hundredths of a degree per second—so the water temperature escalates gradually. Class members check the beaker a couple of hours later, and they find a dead frog. He has boiled to death!

Here's the surprising part. Anyone who keeps his eyes glued to the frog the whole time never sees the creature squirm or try to jump out of the water. The change occurs so slowly that the frog is never aware of it. He never realizes that he's in any danger.

Every time I recall that gruesome demonstration, I think of how gradually a person's attitudes and values can erode. Sin rarely destroys a person's life instantaneously. Rather, the change happens subtly, over a period of time. If we're not careful, we suddenly find ourselves in boiling water with no avenue of escape.

A certain Bible character reminds me of the hapless frog. At first glance, it looks like his fall from the pinnacle of prestige to the quicksand of disgrace was sudden. In the span of a few hours, he vacated the Oval Office of Judah and assumed the role of a despised social outcast. But a closer investigation shows that the underlying cause of his fall from power had been welling up inside him for quite some time. He had a flame flickering in his heart that gradually eroded his character. Then on one unfortunate occasion, it permanently scarred his life.

That flame was *pride*.

Take King Uzziah's story to heart, and you'll save yourself from a lot of hot water.

ROYAL ACHIEVER

Uzziah was king of Judah more than a century before Josiah's birth. At age 16, Uzziah launched a 52-year reign during which the nation enjoyed unparalleled prosperity.

He beefed up the national defense. Under his supervision, Judah boasted an army of 307,500, "who could wage war with great power" (2 Chronicles 26:13, NASB). He invented "engines of war"—contraptions that could catapult arrows and huge stones a long distance. To the west, he routed the Philistine army. To the south, he subdued the Arabs. The Ammonites, nestled along Judah's eastern border, saluted Uzziah's strength, and they wisely decided not to test his army.

Uzziah enjoyed equal success with domestic issues. To increase agricultural output, he devised an elaborate irrigation system. Unemployment plummeted to an all-time low as he encouraged construction of new towers and cities.

God's Word clearly tells what accounted for those decades of unblemished success. Sure, Uzziah possessed uncanny wisdom, exceptional administrative gifts, and military know-how. But here's the real reason for his prosperity: "As long as he sought the Lord, God gave him success" (26:15).

Throughout the early years of his rule, Uzziah relied heavily on a religious adviser named Zechariah. Zechariah tutored him and encouraged him to seek the Lord for the insight needed to guide the country. As a result, Uzziah "did what was right in the eyes of the Lord" (26:4).

His reliance on the Lord was tested, though, by the praise he received. As you can guess, his fame was widespread. Uzziah's exploits earned him gaudy press clippings and international acclaim. That's when the flame of pride first began to flicker and the slow erosion of his character began. He apparently spent too much time dwelling on his achievements.

THE PERIL OF PRIDE

Perhaps the jam-packed schedule of an executive took its toll on the king's devotional life, leaving him vulnerable to the subtle attack of pride. We aren't told *how* it happened. But we are told that he became addicted to the narcotic of self-importance.

Arrogance penetrated a chink in the king's armor:

> So he became very famous, for the Lord helped him wonderfully until he was very powerful. But at that point he became proud—and corrupt. He sinned against

> the Lord his God by entering the forbid-
> den sanctuary of the Temple and person-
> ally burning incense upon the altar.
>   *2 Chronicles 26:15-16*, TLB

Back in the Old Testament era, the temple was the worship center for the Jews. God had prescribed an elaborate system of religious rituals as a means of worshiping Him and confessing sin. One clear-cut stipulation was that *only the priests* could burn incense in the temple on behalf of the people. Not even the king had this privilege. Uzziah was familiar with that divine decree, but he blatantly disregarded it and usurped the priests' function.

A band of 81 priests tried to restrain him. They said, "It is not for you, Uzziah, to burn incense. That is the work of the priests alone. . . . Get out, for you have trespassed, and the Lord is not going to honor you for this!" (26:18, TLB) But their warnings were ignored. "Uzziah was furious, and refused to set down the incense burner he was holding" (26:19, TLB).

The king paid an inflated price for flaunting God's law. While he was arguing with the priests, leprosy broke out on his forehead. And God claimed direct responsibility for it.

Leprosy is a chronic disease that results in loss of sensation in the body's network of nerves. It causes ugly splotches to appear on the skin, and can lead to gross physical deformities. Among the Jews, persons with leprosy were physical and social outcasts. Lepers were forced to separate themselves from family and friends, and they were denied the privileges of a normal lifestyle.

Just like that, the Lord toppled Uzziah's regime. Uzziah was shuttled into exile, and Judah inaugurated a new king. There's no indication that he ever felt sorry for his rash act of disobedience. He lived as a leper the rest of his life.

Let's put Uzziah's story under our mental microscopes. What prevailing lessons can we learn? What principles apply to us today?

TEST RESULTS

When you hear the phrase "test of faith," what pops into your mind?

Most folks imagine some adverse circumstance: a life threatening illness, a nosedive in income, rejection by a significant person, or a nagging temptation to sin. No doubt about it—those circumstances test a person's faith in Jesus Christ. Believe it or not, though, *prosperity is an even stiffer test of our faith and commitment to the Lord.* Most of us can handle a hard time better than some eye-popping achievement or promotion.

Uzziah dramatically illustrates that fact. Over the years, economic and military prosperity bred in him a spirit of self-sufficiency. The more he achieved, the less he nurtured a walk with God, and the less credit he gave to God. He overestimated his own role in his success, and underestimated God's involvement. Uzziah failed the faith test. He shifted his reliance away from God, to the natural abilities God had given him. He forgot that "every good and perfect gift is from above, coming down from the Father" (James 1:17).

No matter what imperfections you see in your personal makeup and circumstances, you have some assets that could cause a proud spirit. Do others envy your looks or athletic ability? Do they wish they could swap their grades or SAT scores for yours? Do your folks earn enough to provide you with a car, all the clothes you want, or an education at the college of your choice? Can you sing or play an instrument? Can you paint or write with a flair?

What is your attitude toward your assets? Is your heart thankful to the Lord? Or do your gifts inject the poison of self-importance into your system? Are you humbled by the increased responsibility you have before God as a steward of your resources? Or do you falsely equate your abilities and assets with your value as a person?

Hammer this point deep into your consciousness: *There's absolutely nothing wrong with such blessings. It's one's attitude toward prosperity and achievement that makes all the difference.* Mulling over these words can help cultivate the right attitude:

> This is what the Lord says: "Let not the wise man boast of his wisdom or the strong man boast of his strength or the rich man boast of his riches, but let him who boasts boast about this: that he understands and knows Me, that I am the Lord, who exercises kindness, justice and righteousness on earth, for in these I delight," declares the Lord.
> *Jeremiah 9:23-24*

I once saw a TV ad produced by a sporting goods manufacturer. The company was touting a tennis racket that Jimmy Connors had used in the prestigious Wimbledon tournament. The ad showed Connors zigzagging all over the court, slapping the tennis ball across the net toward a befuddled opponent. Then an announcer's voice boasted, *"Our racket won Wimbledon."*

When you stop and think about it, that was a pompous and ridiculous claim. I thought all along that Jimmy Connors had won that tournament. I've never heard of a tennis racket that had its own trophy room!

Here's the crunch. Who deserved the sports page accolades—Jimmy Connors, or the tennis racket? Did that racket win Wimbledon, with assistance from Jimmy Connors? Or did Jimmy Connors win Wimbledon, with the racket's help?

Getting proud over our abilities and achievements is almost as foolish as Connors' tennis racket demanding an interview with the press and asking for half of the tournament's cash prize. King Uzziah learned the hard way that the one who controls the racket should get the credit. God deserved the praise for Uzziah's success.

DOMINO EFFECT

Have you ever played with dominoes? If you line up those little blocks with just the right intervening spaces, you can topple all of them with a slight push on the first one. One fallen chip leads to another, then another, and so on.

That's the kind of effect some sins have. Unless we quickly confess them, they cause a chain reaction that erodes a character, destroys relationships, or topples a promising career. One sin often leads to another.

For example, a teacher confronts a student suspected of cheating on a paper. The guilty student escapes immediate punishment because he lies to cover up the cheating. Or a guy makes a habit of browsing through pornographic magazines, becoming increasingly engrossed in the X-rated pictures.

Pretty soon, he coaxes his girlfriend into going all the way. Sin has escalated.

If you could line up the 15 or 20 most notorious sins domino style, which would you put first? Which sin most frequently sets other sins in motion, serving as the catalyst for a downward moral spiral?

You guessed it—*pride.* Uzziah's story should blaze a warning in our minds about its devastating effects. His defiance of God's law about burning incense came *after* pride surfaced over his accomplishments. God's Word even says that Uzziah's moral erosion stemmed from his arrogance: "But after Uzziah became powerful, his pride led to his downfall. He was unfaithful to the Lord his God" (2 Chronicles 26:16).

This cause and effect factor is what makes pride so hazardous. Pride caused Uzziah to neglect his walk with God. That gradually hardened his heart and made him more vulnerable to other temptations that Satan threw at him. Before long, he felt he could disobey God's laws and get away with it. Eventually there wasn't a piece of his life that hadn't been toppled by the movement of that first domino.

How vividly he illustrated the truth of Proverbs 18:12: "Before his downfall a man's heart is proud." Somebody else put it this way: "Some folks pay so much attention to their reputation that they lose their character."

THE FINISH LINE

Do you remember how the Bible described King Josiah's life? "He did what was right in the eyes of the Lord . . . not turning aside to the right or to the left" (2 Chronicles 34:2). Throughout a 31-year reign, he stuck to the spiritual commitment he had made as a teenager. He finished his life with the

"What do you mean this is a marathon!
I thought it was a 100-yard dash!"

same spiritual zeal he had in the early days.

Not Uzziah. He started off on the right foot, all right. But he wasn't consistent over the long haul. He didn't realize that *how we finish is more important than how we start*. He had a spurt of religious commitment, but faltered before the finish line. Perhaps Uzziah expected a 100-yard dash, only to discover that one's faith is tested by a grueling marathon!

Junk any idea that you have arrived spiritually because of a one-time experience with the Lord. Maybe you were sincere when you made that commitment at camp or on a retreat. If so, that gave you an ironclad reservation in heaven. But conversion itself doesn't insulate you from temptation or the possibility of moral failure. Lots of Christians have scarred their lives and rendered themselves useless to the Lord because they got lazy. They stopped tapping into God's power through Bible study and prayer. They pulled away from faith-strengthening fellowship with the church youth group. They took spiritual warfare for granted, and wound up victims instead of victors. One of the most sobering facts about the Christian life is that it's so *daily*.

Perhaps Uzziah faltered because he never had a healthy, *independent* relationship with the Lord. Was he excessively dependent on Zechariah, his spiritual adviser? Apparently, he sought the Lord only in the days of Zechariah (26:5).

Have I touched a nerve? Have you honestly made your own gut-level decision to follow the Lord, or are you trying to get by on your parents' faith? Are you attending church youth activities solely to gain the affection of someone else in the group? Do you go through the motions of studying God's Word, praying, and singing in order to identify with the group?

Or in addition to the legitimate social attraction, is there a rock-ribbed personal faith in Christ that motivates you? Before you ask another Christian to pray for a particular need, do you close the door to your room and plead your case before God in private?

Make no mistake about it. In order to finish strong, we need the help of other Christians. But their support isn't enough if we aren't also nurturing a private, independent walk with the Lord.

King Uzziah literally sat on a throne. The elevated throne was an elaborately constructed chair, often covered by a canopy that symbolized a position of supreme rank in the country. Ironically, his downfall began when he shoved God off the throne of his heart, and began ruling his own life.

A throne has a seating capacity of only one. I don't know about you, but I feel much safer when God is running things—not me.

THE MAN WITH THE MIGHTY MOUTH

Acts 18:24-28;
1 Corinthians 1:10-12; 3:3-9

———

Recently I came across some belly-tickling quotes published in the July 26, 1977 issue of the *Toronto News*. These are actual statements from auto insurance claim forms. Drivers were attempting to explain the cause of their accidents in as few words as possible. They weren't trying to be comical, but what they actually communicated strayed a bit from what they intended to say.

● "I thought my car window was down, but I found out it was up when I put my head through it."

● "A truck backed through my windshield and into my wife's face."

● "A pedestrian hit me and went under my car."

● "The guy was all over the road. I had to swerve a number of times before I hit him."

● "I pulled away from the side of the road, glanced at my mother-in-law, and headed over the embankment."

● "I had been driving for 40 years when I fell asleep at the wheel and had an accident."

● "I told the police that I was not injured, but

upon removing my hair, I found that I had a frac-
tured skull."

● "I was sure the old fellow would never make it
to the other side of the road when I struck him."

● "The pedestrian had no idea which direction to
run, so I ran over him."

● "I saw a slow-moving, sad-faced old gentleman
as he bounced off the hood of my car."

● "I was thrown from my car as it left the road. I
was later found in a ditch by some stray cows."

● "The telephone pole was approaching. I was
attempting to swerve out of its way when it struck
my front end."

● "My car was legally parked as it backed into the
other vehicle."

That shows what can happen when communication
is fuzzy. Whether we're writing a letter, chatting on
the phone, taking an essay test, or giving a speech,
clear communication is vital. The message we want
to get across needs to be perceived correctly in the
minds of recipients—or else accurate communication
hasn't taken place.

Allow me to introduce you to perhaps the most
incisive communicator mentioned in Scripture. When
he wrote term papers, clichés never cluttered the
pages. When he spoke, his words jabbed the minds
of his hearers and cut through their complacency.
He was a "word carpenter" who constructed an
effective public ministry for Jesus Christ. I call him
"the man with the mighty mouth." His name was
Apollos.

Why does Apollos deserve such a tribute? What
made him an effective communicator of his faith in
Jesus Christ? What traits did he have that Christians
of all eras desperately need? We'll answer those
questions in the next few pages.

DR. APOLLOS

Apollos grew up in Alexandria, the cultural and educational capital of first-century Egypt. He received a thorough education in both the Jewish Scriptures (Old Testament) and Greek classical literature. His formal training probably earned him the equivalent of today's Ph.D.

After he heard and accepted the Good News of Jesus Christ, he funneled his newfound spiritual zeal into full-time work as an evangelist and teacher. In order to establish churches and bolster the faith of young Christians who faced persecution, Apollos often worked elbow-to-elbow with better-known leaders like the Apostle Paul.

Acts 18:24-28 tells about the time he entered the city of Ephesus. There he beefed up the work already started by Paul and a married couple named Aquila and Priscilla. When these believers first heard him speak, they were no doubt impressed by his oratory and enthusiasm. But one thing alarmed them. What Apollos knew, he taught accurately. But despite having a scholar's grasp of the Old Testament, there were gaps in his knowledge about Christ. Oh, he knew the basics. He was convinced Jesus was the promised Messiah. Yet he wasn't familiar with all the details concerning Christ's three-year public ministry, death, and resurrection. He hadn't spent much time in and around Jerusalem when Christ was ministering. Some helpful information had escaped him.

TEACHER TURNED STUDENT

Aquila and Priscilla resolved this dilemma by inviting Apollos to their home to tell him what they knew about Jesus. They saw eyebrow-raising potential in Apollos. They knew that the added information would improve an already fruitful ministry.

Remember—Apollos' formal education far exceeded that of Aquila and Priscilla. Their grasp of the Old Testament probably paled in comparison to his. And compared to Apollos' eloquence, their verbal skills were at the kindergarten level. Despite these areas in which Apollos was head-and-shoulders above them, he listened intently to their instruction. He wasn't threatened or defensive. Like a sponge, his mind soaked up the details about Christ.

Not long after this fireside chat with Aquila and Priscilla, Apollos sailed to Corinth in Achaia. The Corinthians had first heard the Gospel from Paul. When Apollos arrived, "he was a great help to those who by grace had believed" (Acts 18:27). On top of his teaching ministry to young Christians, Apollos publicly debated unbelieving Jews. Like a scalpel, his words cut deeply into their hearts. He was "proving from the Scriptures that Jesus was the Christ" (18:28). Think of it—his mastery of the Old Testament blended perfectly with the instruction about Jesus that he had received from Aquila and Priscilla. When he got flak from skeptics, his arguments were irrefutable.

But a few immature Christians in Corinth were *too* awed by Apollos' eloquence. We find in 1 Corinthians 1:10-12 that they began exalting *him* rather than Jesus Christ. Other leaders encountered the same problem. One group rallied around Peter; another band of believers followed Paul.

Members of each clique considered themselves more spiritual because of the particular leader they followed. The result was division that threatened the spiritual health of the church. There was never friction over the matter among Apollos, Paul, and Peter.

And none of these men encouraged such a competitive atmosphere. In fact, to see their names eclipsing the Son of God from the heart of the Corinthians broke their own hearts. To resolve the issue, Paul wrote the church a letter:

> What, after all, is Apollos? And what is Paul? Only servants, through whom you came to believe—as the Lord has assigned to each his task. I planted the seed, Apollos watered it, but God made it grow. So neither he who plants nor he who waters is anything, but only God, who makes things grow.
>
> *1 Corinthians 3:5-7*

Now let's analyze this portrait of Apollos in Scripture. Take a closer look, and you'll notice three features that God wants to blend into your life and mine.

A KNOWLEDGEABLE MIND

The first striking feature we see in Apollos is a *mind saturated with the Word of God*. "He was a learned man, with a thorough knowledge of the Scriptures" (Acts 18:24).

Have you ever heard speakers whose oratory was well-polished, yet who never seemed to say anything? Not Apollos. To a God-given flair for public speaking, he added diligent study. Having something to say—not just the ability to say it—made him a spellbinding communicator. For him, public presentation was always preceded by private preparation. His mind was a storehouse for the Word.

No matter what vocational choice you make, one

key to your usefulness as a Christian is your grasp of Scripture. Do you know enough of God's truth to combat skeptics who mock your commitment to Christ? To comfort a hurting friend? To make decisions based on spiritual rather than cultural values? Can you use your Bible to show an inquiring friend how to receive Christ as Saviour?

Such a working knowledge of God's Word doesn't require a Bible college diploma. But it does require you to make Bible study a regular habit. Peter pulled no punches when he wrote, "In your hearts set apart Christ as Lord. Always be prepared to give an answer to everyone who asks you to give the reason for the hope that you have" (1 Peter 3:15).

God's written Word has power that no other literature can match. When we share it—through a testimony, in a letter, as a teacher, etc.—the Holy Spirit energizes it in the mind of the hearer or reader. The recipient can choose to resist God's wooing, but the potential to change his life is present. Let God's Word speak for itself:

God to Joshua:

> Do not let this Book of the Law depart from your mouth; meditate on it day and night, so that you may be careful to do everything written in it. Then you will be prosperous and successful.
> *Joshua 1:8*

Paul to Timothy:

> From infancy you have known the holy Scriptures, which are able to make you wise for salvation through faith in Christ Jesus. All Scripture is God-breathed and

is useful for teaching, rebuking, correcting and training in righteousness, so that the man of God may be thoroughly equipped for every good work.
2 Timothy 3:15-17

The writer to the Hebrews:

The word of God is living and active. Sharper than any double-edged sword, it penetrates even to dividing soul and spirit, joints and marrow; it judges the thoughts and attitudes of the heart.
Hebrews 4:12

An Associated Press story dated January 9, 1986 told about an 89-year-old Pennsylvania recluse who froze to death in his unheated home. Gas service to his house had been cut off two years prior to his death. Near his body, authorities found an unplugged space heater. There was only one electric light bulb in the house, and no television or radio.

It sounds like the all-too-familiar story of a poverty-stricken retiree. Except they found $188,000 in cash stashed in his house, plus thousands more in assets willed to a church he seldom attended. The coroner who investigated the death said, "I can't understand why a person of his means would choose to live like that."

God's bank of spiritual resources is open 24 hours a day for withdrawals. Will the riches of His Word, which He has deposited in your account, go unclaimed? Or will your heart grow so cold that someone says about you, "I can't understand why a person of his means would choose to live like that"?

A ZEALOUS HEART

Further examination of Apollos' portrait unveils *a zealous heart*. To his vast knowledge he added a contagious enthusiasm, a zest for the Lord's work that proved he really believed what he preached.

According to Acts 18:25, "he spoke with great fervor." The word "fervor" means "bubbling" or "boiling over." He was so excited about what the Lord had done for him that he couldn't keep the lid on it. His message burned like fire in his bones. The verb translated "spoke" carries the idea of continuous action. Apollos made a habit of talking about Jesus. Witnessing was a lifestyle for him, not just a profession to exercise from 9:00 to 5:00. His gusto for the Gospel was deeply rooted, far from a pep rally kind of fanaticism that wanes in a few hours.

A mind stuffed with God's Word is useless without a warm heart. How did Apollos keep his heart tender and maintain his spiritual enthusiasm over the years?

First, he kept short accounts with God. When he sinned, he confessed it right away. He knew that trying to cover up his mistakes would bring energy-sapping results. King David learned that lesson in the schoolroom of experience:

> When I kept silent, my bones wasted away through my groaning all day long. For day and night Your hand was heavy upon me; my strength was sapped as in the heat of summer. Then I acknowledged my sin to You and did not cover up my iniquity. I said, "I will confess my transgressions to the Lord"—and You forgave the guilt of my sin.
> *Psalm 32:3-6*

Second, Apollos digested God's Word for personal benefit. He didn't use it merely as a textbook or teacher's manual. He didn't pore over it merely to find insights to dump on a public audience. No doubt he prayed over what he read, and first applied it to himself. Apollos didn't fall into the trap of peddling God's Word without enjoying it. Because he kept his eye on the Person who inspired the Scriptures, icicles never had a chance to form on his heart.

Remember Eric Liddell? He was the 1924 Olympic champion whose story was told in the film *Chariots of Fire*. He served as a missionary in China for a couple decades after earning headlines for his running exploits. In the early 1940s, he was whisked away to a Japanese prison camp, where he died shortly before World War II ended.

Survivors of that camp claim that his zeal for Jesus Christ never waned during the hardships of those years. He organized sports activities for children, eagerly performed mundane chores such as carrying buckets of coal, and led Bible studies for other prisoners. Here are comments made by some of his companions:

● "His smile was infectious."

● "He was without a doubt the person most in demand and most respected and loved in camp."

● "In camp he was in his middle forties, lithe and springy of step and, above all, overflowing with good humor and love of life."

How did he maintain his spiritual gusto in such a deprived environment? A woman whose husband lived with Liddell in that camp came up with this answer:

> Every morning about 6 A.M., with curtains tightly drawn to keep in the shining

of our peanut-oil lamp, lest the prowling sentries would think someone was trying to escape, he used to climb out of his top bunk, past the sleeping forms of his dormitory mates. Then, at the small Chinese table, the two men would sit close together with the light just enough to illumine their Bibles and notebooks. Silently they read, prayed, thought about the day's duties, noted what should be done. Eric was a man of prayer not only at set times—though he did not like to miss a prayer meeting or communion service when such could be arranged. He talked to God all the time, naturally, as one can who enters the "school of prayer" to learn this way of inner discipline. He seemed to have no weighty mental problems: his life was grounded in God, in faith, and in trust. (Sally Magnusson, *The Flying Scotsman*, Quartet Books, p. 165)

Liddell's heart could have grown cold in that camp, but he maintained a vibrant relationship with Christ that made him sensitive to the needs of those around him.

Above his large fireplace a homeowner framed these words: "If Your Heart Is Cold, My Fire Cannot Warm It." Apollos would nod in agreement. Crackling fireplaces can't keep a heart warm and zestful. Only an intimate walk with the Lord can.

A HUMBLE SPIRIT

Don't take your eyes off Apollos' portrait yet. Perhaps the most outstanding feature is his

"OK, so Apollos is a great speaker, he knows the Scripture inside out, and he's even got a warm heart. I suppose *now* you're going to tell me he's *humble* too. . . ."

humility. Neither his prestigious education, his verbal eloquence, nor the success he enjoyed in ministry went to his head. Unlike King Uzziah (see chapter 4), he passed the test which giftedness and prosperity posed to his faith. The bite of pride never spread its deadly venom into his bloodstream.

Though he was better educated and more talented than Aquila and Priscilla, Apollos welcomed their criticism and instruction. He realized that no one ever has it all together. On top of that, long after he had served in Corinth, Paul urged Apollos to visit the city again. But he refused. Some of his devotees in Corinth had previously put him on a pedestal. Apollos didn't want to steal any of the glory that he knew belonged to Jesus Christ.

Without an attitude like Apollos had—of dependency on others, an appetite to increase his knowledge and sharpen his skills, and an openness to constructive criticism—we'll never tap our potential for Jesus Christ. It was no less of a theologian than Charlie Brown who said, "There's no heavier burden than great potential."

Perhaps the clearest indicator of humility, or the lack of it, is how we handle criticism. Apollos' responsiveness to Aquila and Priscilla reminds me of what author Gordon MacDonald said about handling criticism:

> Growth always comes when we also *listen to our critics*. And that is not an easy thing for any of us to do. Dawson Trotman, the founder of the Navigators, had a good method for handling all criticisms directed at himself. No matter how unfair the criticism might seem to be, he would always take it into his prayer closet and in

effect spread it before the Lord. Then he would say, "Lord, please show me the kernel of truth hidden in this criticism." (*Ordering Your Private World*, expanded edition, Oliver-Nelson, pp. 105-106)

Apollos didn't blow his stack in Aquila and Priscilla's living room, perhaps because he had memorized such verses as Proverbs 12:1: "Whoever loves discipline loves knowledge, but he who hates correction is stupid." Or Proverbs 17:10: "A rebuke goes deeper into one who has understanding than a hundred blows into a fool" (NASB).

Receiving criticism from a parent, coach, teacher, or peer is like sitting on a tack: if the point is on target, there's no painless way to manage it. In a *Campus Life* article titled "Nobody Loves a Critic" (December 1978), Lew Allen offers useful techniques on accepting it in an Apollos-like manner:

● *Listen to the criticism.* Don't interrupt. Let your critic know you're listening by looking directly at him or her.

● *Never launch a counterattack.* There's no point in criticizing your critic in response to his complaints—even if you feel his criticism is unjust. That shifts attention away from the point the other person is trying to make.

● *Don't joke.* If you react flippantly to what is already a serious and unpleasant atmosphere, you'll project an attitude of contempt.

● *Don't exaggerate the complaint.* If a friend says he felt you were thoughtless one time, don't read into it that he means you're an insensitive clod and then defend yourself against a charge he never made.

● *Whether you agree with it or not, let the other person know that you understand his complaint.*

Restating or paraphrasing the criticism is a good way to do this.

• *Don't accuse your critic of some hostile motive for his complaint.*

• *Try to set your critic at ease.* Thank him or her for caring enough to approach you. If you need to apologize, do it first thing. The longer you wait, the harder it is.

• *Later, mull over what was said.* Ask the Lord to show you whether the other person has a valid point.

As you can see, a teachable spirit is a sign of strength. There's nothing wimpy about it. That's why so few can respond responsibly to criticism.

COMMUNICATING CHANGE

Are you a *thermometer,* or a *thermostat?* A thermometer doesn't change anything around it—it just registers the temperature. It's always going up and down. In contrast, a thermostat regulates the surroundings and changes them when they need to be changed. Do you experience spiritual ups and downs as the situations change around you? Or are you the kind of person who, controlled by God's Spirit, regulates and influences your circumstances?

Follow the example of Apollos. A mind teeming with Scripture, a zealous heart, and a humble spirit can make you into a thermostat—a person who can change the world by boldly communicating the Good News of Christ.

WHEN GOD CALLS, DON'T HANG UP

Jonah 1:1–2:10

———

Have you ever deliberately disobeyed the law?

Probably. Chances are, though, that you've *unintentionally* broken civil laws even more frequently. In some states, there are a few wacky ordinances still officially on the books, carryovers from a bygone era. The next time you travel and your stomach starts growling, beware of the following food laws:

• In the Commonwealth of Massachusetts, it's against the law to eat peanuts in church or to use tomatoes in making clam chowder.

• In New Jersey, authorities can arrest you for slurping soup in a public restaurant.

• An old Kansas ordinance forbids you from eating snakes on Sunday, or rattlesnake meat in public.

• In Waterloo, Nebraska, barbers can't eat onions between 7 A.M. and 7 P.M.

• When you visit Lexington, Kentucky, eat your ice-cream cone at one sitting. The law says you can't carry it in your pocket.

• A long time ago, a sham artist must have duped the folks in LeHigh, Nebraska. They wrote a regulation outlawing the sale of doughnut holes.

● Pickle lovers, take note. In Connecticut, pickles which collapse in their own juice are illegal. When dropped 12 inches or more, the pickles must remain whole—and even bounce.

● In Green, New York, you can't eat peanuts and walk backward on the sidewalk during a concert.

Even if you flout some of these statutes, the police probably won't nab you. Technically, they could throw the book at you. But odds are in your favor that no one will press charges.

God's laws are a different matter—they don't go out of date. Disregarding His regulations for living is no laughing matter. This chapter zeroes in on a man who deliberately ducked out of a divine command. What happened to him speaks volumes about the consequences of detouring around God's will.

When biblical history speaks, let's perk our ears and listen. Accounts of characters like *Jonah* are chock-full of helpful insights for today.

THE FUGITIVE

Back in the eighth century B.C., Jonah was a prominent prophet in Israel. A prophet was a specially called leader who received direct revelations from God in response to a crisis or need on earth. Then the prophet had the job of conveying God's message to the masses. Normally, God geared prophetic messages to the Jewish people, to whom He had given the Law, in order to jar them out of a state of complacency or disobedience.

In Jonah's case, God shucked the normal routine. He told Jonah to sail 500 miles to the east and drop a warning on the inhabitants of Nineveh so they would repent.

If Jonah only knew. . . .

Jonah balked. The new assignment was as taste-
less to him as last year's gum stuck beneath the
church pew. He bought a one-way ticket to Tarshish,
a Spanish port 2,000 miles to the west.

Why did Jonah shun this particular mission? Nineveh was the capital of Assyria. The Assyrians,
dreaded enemies of the Jews, had an international
reputation for terrorism. Any prophet told to warn
those folks about God's judgment would need ice
water in his veins. In *Real Characters in the Making*
(Bethany), Lorraine Peterson paints a savage portrait of this Middle Eastern nation:

> They skinned people alive. They buried
> men up to their necks in the hot desert
> sand, put holes in their tongues, and let
> them bake to death. They used men's
> heads as decorations for their garden par-
> ties. They had made raids into Israel, so
> they may have killed friends or relatives
> of Jonah. (p. 162)

The last thing Jonah wanted was for God to forgive
the Ninevites. He wanted them to get what they
deserved—punishment, not pardon. He knew God
was just the type to send a revival and let them off
the hook, and he wanted no part of it.

Yet God stayed right on Jonah's heels. He sent a
violent storm that scared the wits out of the ship's
crew. The sailors begged their false gods for help,
but to no avail. Jonah knew God was trying to get his
attention. "Throw me overboard," he insisted, "and
the storm will stop."

Jonah expected to drown in the Mediterranean
Sea. To him, death was more attractive than obedience. But there's one thing he didn't count on. When

an individual fails, God doesn't abandon His plans for that person.

God implemented a peculiar rescue operation. He "provided a great fish to swallow Jonah, and Jonah was inside the fish three days and three nights" (Jonah 1:17). While on a tour of the fish's digestive tract, Jonah came to his senses. He spit out seaweed and salt water long enough to confess his defiance and reapply for His prophet's license.

A lot of folks find it hard to swallow this part of the story. The facts seem to defy logic. It isn't the most important part of Jonah's story, but since it's the place where most readers go under, let's spend some time on it.

BELIEVE IT—OR NOT

Lots of old yarns about seamen surviving in the belly of a fish have made the rounds. But at least one has its roots in fact. Researcher David Gunston wrote, "In a long and close study of the subject I have discovered only one instance completely corroborated by reliable authorities, and its details are so remarkable that it is worth recounting" (*Compass*, Spring 1972, pp. 10-11).

In her discussion of Jonah, Lorraine Peterson summarizes Gunston's research:

The victim was David Bartly.

In February, 1891, Bartly was aboard the *Star of the East*, an English whaling ship searching near the Falkland Islands for oil-rich sperm whales about 60-70 ft. long. Upon spotting a whale, the crew gave chase in two small boats. One harpooner speared the whale in the side, and during the ensuing struggle, the other boat overturned. One man drowned, and a later check revealed that Bartly was missing.

After killing the whale, crewmen secured it to the side of their ship and began to cut the huge creature apart. The next morning as they prepared to cut open the stomach, it moved! Mystified, they opened it and found fellow-crewmember, David Bartly, "doubled up, drenched, but still alive though deeply unconscious." His face and hands had been bleached white by the whale's gastric juices. The men soaked him with sea water and put him to bed in the captain's cabin. At first delirious, within three weeks Bartly recovered. When recounting the experience, Bartly said breathing was no problem, but he found his "prison" terribly hot. (The body temperature of a whale is 104 degrees F.) Bartly continued his life as a sailor and apparently avoided publicity.

David Bartly's experience has been authenticated by fellow crew members and investigated by . . . [scholars who] concluded the story was accurate.

David Bartly's ordeal doesn't prove a man could live three days and three nights inside a whale without miraculous intervention. After all, Bartly was not inside the whale as long as Jonah was, and Bartly's whale was dead part of that time. Nonetheless, the incident should squelch people who categorize the account of Jonah and the whale with *Gulliver's*

Travels and Little Red Riding Hood. (pp. 160-161)

We shouldn't rely on David Bartly's story, however, to convince us of Jonah's experience. If we believe in the God of the Bible, supernatural events shouldn't throw us for a loop. The God who created natural laws is certainly capable of skirting them occasionally in order to accomplish His purposes.

To stretch this line of reasoning, belief in one miracle—such as creation of the world, or Jesus' resurrection—should pry open our minds to the possibilities of others. Let's face it—miracles go hand in glove with Christianity. Rob Christianity of its miraculous features, and you destroy it.

Besides, Jesus Himself saluted the historical accuracy of Jonah. He compared His impending death and resurrection to Jonah's stay in the fish: "As Jonah was three days and three nights in the belly of a huge fish, so the Son of Man will be three days and three nights in the heart of the earth" (Matthew 12:40). Questioning the historical accuracy of Jonah amounts to doubting the integrity of Jesus Christ as well!

With that episode in Jonah's life out of the way, we can shift our attention to the truths lurking behind the facts. What practical insights can we wring out of this part of his story?

RISKY BUSINESS

Did you hear about the young Christian who prayed about whether or not to cheat on an exam? Or the girl who concluded, "God wouldn't let me fall in love with Tom if He didn't think it was all right to go to bed with him." To top it all off, one fellow reasoned, "God made our bodies, so watching an X-rated videotape on my VCR isn't so bad."

There's something radically wrong with such statements. The persons involved have forgotten that God means what He says. Period. He hasn't published a revised edition of His commands. When we don't take His Word at face value, we get in over our heads. Just ask Jonah!

No amount of rationalizing about circumstances or desires will alter reality. Disobedience is sin, and sin brings painful consequences. Neither the wind-whipped deck of a ship nor the digestive tract of an overgrown fish were comfortable classrooms. Yet that's where God taught Jonah this lesson. What kind of schoolroom will it take to soften our hearts and make us willing to obey?

I recently came across a sobering illustration of this principle. An 18-year-old high school athlete severed his spinal cord in an auto accident. He's permanently paralyzed from the chest down and confined to a wheelchair.

It had snowed and rained a lot the night before the accident. Icy roads had caused a rash of fender benders in the area. Despite the weather conditions, he and an older friend who lived nearby decided to go out. The boy's parents reluctantly gave their OK— except they emphatically said he couldn't do the driving or use his car.

Later, he and his pal sneaked back to his house and took the car anyway. The gleeful 18-year-old took the wheel. Heading for a party at 60 miles per hour, the front tires hit a sheet of ice, flinging the car 100 feet into the air. The boy defied his parents—and you already know the results. In that instance, old-fashioned obedience would have helped him a lot more than seat belts.

I'll admit that consequences of wrongdoing aren't always that sudden or severe. But with the severity of a submachine gun, God's Word warns us against a flippant attitude toward disobedience: "Do not be deceived: God cannot be mocked. A man reaps what he sows. The one who sows to please his sinful nature, from that nature will reap destruction; the one who sows to please the Spirit, from the Spirit will reap eternal life" (Galatians 6:7-8).

All this talk about obedience shouldn't cloud the fact that God loves us *as we are*—not just so long as we stay clean behind the ears. In fact, love for us is what motivates the Lord to give us regulations. Because He's a loving God, we can view His commands as an invitation to experience His very best. Whenever our disobedience causes us pain, He hurts too. This perspective helps us understand what John meant when he wrote, "His commands are not burdensome" (1 John 5:3).

What's on trial isn't God's character—it's His lordship. Who's calling the shots in our lives? If we know the Lord, there's only one way to prove that His residency is a presidency.

Obedience . . . nothing more, nothing less, nothing else.

Whoa! We aren't through with Jonah's story. The next chapter explains several more principles, and tells what happened after the fish vomited him out on the beach.

A FUGITIVE'S FRESH START

Jonah 3:1–4:11

In a local advertising newspaper, I read the following disclaimer:

> Just in case you find mistakes in this paper, please remember that they were put there for a purpose. Some folks are always looking for mistakes, and we try to please everyone!

Despite our craving for success, man's real genius lies in the opposite direction. When it comes to making mistakes, we're all pros. But a few standout people have mastered the fine art of blowing it. They've put failure in the category of a science. Their mistakes stand head and shoulders above the average blunder. A few such stories are featured in Stephen Pile's *The Incomplete Book of Failures* (E.P. Dutton, pp. 165-167):

● Back in 1962, a Decca record company executive refused to give an upstart British rock group a contract. "We don't like the Beatles' sound," he deadpanned. "Groups with guitars are on their way out."

● Simon Newcomb (1835-1909) quipped, "Flight by machines heavier than air is impractical and insignificant . . . utterly impossible."

● In 1837, music critic Philip Hale blurted, "If Beethoven's Seventh Symphony is not by some means abridged, it will soon fall into disuse."

● Between 1962 and 1977, Arthur Pedrick patented 162 inventions. That sounds impressive, but none of them ever earned him a penny. Why? For example, he planned to irrigate the world's deserts by sending a constant supply of snowballs from the polar region through a massive network of giant pea-shooters.

● During the firemen's strike in England in 1978, the British Army took over emergency fire fighting. On January 14, an elderly lady in South London asked the soldiers to retrieve her cat from a tree. Afterward, the grateful owner invited the troop of heroes in for tea. A few minutes later, waving good-bye, they backed the fire truck over the cat and killed it.

● "You'll never amount to very much." A Munich schoolmaster said that to 10-year-old Albert Einstein.

Pile could have reserved a whole chapter in his book for Jonah, who deliberately failed the Lord. When God ordered him to Nineveh to preach, he gave an emphatic no and hopped on a ship going the opposite direction. As you read in the previous chapter, God pursued Jonah and brought him to his senses. He transferred him to the world's most peculiar cruise ship—the belly of a mammoth fish. That's when Jonah cried uncle, and decided that God's will was more attractive than he originally thought.

The next few pages tell what happened after the

fish spit him up on the beach. Among other things, you'll discover that failure doesn't cramp God's power in your life.

DISCOURAGED BY SUCCESS

Jonah's expulsion from the fish's stomach was grounds for rejoicing. After scrubbing with Lifebuoy for a few hours, he heard God's command a second time: "Go to the great city of Nineveh and proclaim to it the message I give you" (Jonah 3:1).

The actual walled city, which has been unearthed by modern archeologists, was only 2½ miles long and a little over a mile wide. But outside the walls were several population centers, equivalent to today's suburbs. At least 600,000 people populated the total area. For three days, Jonah trudged through the streets. "In 40 days," he announced, "God plans to wipe Nineveh off the map."

God's Spirit cut their hearts to the quick. These wicked people believed in Jonah's God and changed their ways. The king issued a proclamation calling for prayer and fasting. The result? "When God saw what they did and how they turned from their evil ways, He had compassion and did not bring upon them the destruction He had threatened" (3:10).

Having been the catalyst for an earthshaking revival, you'd think Jonah would be ecstatic. Instead, "Jonah was greatly displeased and became angry" (4:1). Then he sank into a rut of depression and longed to die. His ardent patriotism had surfaced again. He admitted, "Lord, these people are our enemies. I hope their repentance fizzles out and You zap them." It may have been the only time in history that a preacher wanted folks to fall asleep during his sermon.

"I may have *said*, 'Repent,' but
what I really *meant* was, 'Die, you
rotten Ninevites!' "

Jonah, still pouting, went out and sat on a hill east of the city. That's when God used peculiar objects and forces of nature to rivet a lesson into Jonah's head. Let's pick up the story:

> Then the Lord God provided a vine and made it grow up over Jonah to give shade for his head to ease his discomfort, and Jonah was very happy about the vine. But at dawn the next day God provided a worm, which chewed the vine so that it withered. When the sun rose, God provided a scorching east wind, and the sun blazed on Jonah's head so that he grew faint. He wanted to die, and said, "It would be better for me to die than to live."
>
> But God said to Jonah, "Do you have a right to be angry about the vine?"
>
> "I do," he said. "I am angry enough to die."
>
> But the Lord said, "You have been concerned about this vine, though you did not tend it or make it grow. It sprang up overnight and died overnight. But Nineveh has more than a hundred and twenty thousand people who cannot tell their right hand from their left [a Hebrew way of describing children], and many cattle as well. Should I not be concerned about that great city?"
>
> *Jonah 4:6-11*

Through that sequence of events, God exposed Jonah's selfishness and lack of spiritual concern. God was saying, "I have a heart of compassion. I love the people in that city just as much as I love the folks back in Israel. I wanted them to repent, but you're all bent out of shape because I forgave them and took away your shade. You care more about sitting in the shade than you care about the souls of those people. Get your priorities in shape!"

We aren't sure how Jonah responded to God's rebuke. The book ends abruptly. But the fact that Jonah wrote the whole story so honestly is a good indication that he straightened things out.

Now let's put the spotlight on a few more practical applications from Jonah's story.

FRESH CHANCES

If Hollywood made a movie of Jonah's story and employed the original cast of characters, the starring role would go to God. Jonah deserves no more than an Academy Award nomination as best *supporting* actor.

One thing the film would vividly portray is God's willingness to give those who fail a second chance (and a third, and a fourth . . .). No one is booted to the unemployment line in God's kingdom just because he shows up late for work once. Despite his brash defiance, Jonah received another opportunity to evangelize the Ninevites.

When we Christians blow it, Satan wants to get us so wrapped up in our failure that we question our status before God. He tries to squelch our prayer life by whispering, "You're too unworthy to enter God's presence. You're the last person God wants to see right now." Jonah's cry from the belly of a fish reminds us that we have access to God even when we've grossly sinned. "In my distress I called to the Lord," Jonah remembered, "and He answered me"

(2:1). When Jonah dialed the Lord's number, there was no static on the line. The author of Hebrews put it this way:

> Jesus the Son of God is our great High Priest who has gone to heaven itself to help us; therefore let us never stop trusting Him. This High Priest of ours understands our weaknesses, since He had the same temptations we do, though He never once gave way to them and sinned. So let us come boldly to the very throne of God and stay there to receive His mercy and to find grace to help us in our times of need.
>
> *Hebrews 4:14-16,* TLB

Do you currently live outside the city limits of God's will? Do drugs or alcohol have you in a pythonic grip? Are you involved in a dating relationship which has gotten out of control? Are you in the habit of cheating on exams or swiping things from department stores? Satan whispers, "You don't have what it takes to follow Jesus Christ. You might as well give up." But Jonah butts in and exclaims, "Don't listen to him. You too can know the God of the second chance."

There's only one catch. As Lorraine Peterson puts it, "You have to go to Nineveh—stop taking drugs, or break off the relationship, or pay back the money you stole. That is real repentance. . . . God won't make any deals. He expects obedience on the very issue that kept you from God's will in the first place. There is no other way to get right with God" (*Real Characters in the Making,* p. 170).

God doles out fresh chances, all right. But we must

be so disgusted with the status quo that we grab them like a starving man who is offered fresh bread. All God wants is to hear us say, "Lord, I've acted foolishly. I'll march to Your drumbeat." It's never too late to do what is right.

WORLD VISION

The punch line of Jonah's script is *God's love for unsaved people.* Because God had initiated a special relationship with the Jewish people, they were vulnerable to the germs of bigotry. They often forgot what God had told the head of their race, Abraham: "All peoples on earth will be blessed through you" (Genesis 12:3). All along, God intended for the Jews to spread His love to Gentiles. His love has no geographical borders or race restrictions.

It's easy for us to point a finger at Jonah and the Israelites. But haven't some germs of prejudice seeped into *our* bloodstreams too? If we could write our own version of John 3:16, would it read, "For God so loved the *middle-class, Anglo-Saxon North Americans,* that He gave His only Son"? Would we crow in triumph if tomorrow's paper reported that Moscow lay in smoldering ruins? Probably. Yet the Lord "wants *all* men to be saved and to come to a knowledge of the truth" (1 Timothy 2:4, italics added).

"All" includes Russians, Arabs, Chinese, Mexicans—you name it. "All" also embraces the unsaved in your own school and community, even those whose behavior is godless and revolting. We sing "Amazing Grace" on Sundays, yet tend to dismiss the "Ninevites" from our lives. But God doesn't dismiss them. He died for them. The circumference of His love is as big as the globe.

PRIZE RECRUITS

You trivia buffs might be interested in the various things God employed in the Book of Jonah to accomplish His work.

The *wind* and other elements of the *storm* promptly responded when God said to rattle the ship (1:4). When God told the *fish* to swallow Jonah whole, it didn't talk back (1:17). Neither did the *vine* which shaded Jonah, the *worm* that chewed the plant, nor the *sun* and *scorching wind* that baked Jonah's scalp (4:6-8).

Ironically, the *human being* was the only divine instrument that dug in its heels and refused to cooperate.

The human being, though, was the *only* instrument used to spread God's message of love and repentance. Other creatures and forces of nature do His bidding. Yet He only communicates the Gospel through *human channels*. Unless God's people tell them, the "Ninevites" on our planet won't hear about the Lord.

A misconception that many people hold about Christianity is that it's *boring*. They perceive that all the real action is in the worlds of business, sports, or entertainment. That shows how little they know about the Bible.

No believer in the will of God leads a boring existence. No siree! That's because God's purpose for *every* Christian includes participation in His grand work in the world. No matter what vocation we choose, God wants us to make a spiritual impact in our spheres of influence. That impact may be through witnessing, teaching, giving money to mission projects—the scope of ways to reach Nineveh is endless! But lack of involvement isn't an option.

Need proof that God doesn't reserve His work just

for the paid staff members of your church? Check out these passages:

> We are God's workmanship, created in Christ Jesus to do good works, which God prepared in advance for us to do.
> *Ephesians 2:10*

> If anyone is in Christ, he is a new creation; the old has gone, the new has come! All this is from God, who reconciled us to Himself through Christ and gave us the ministry of reconciliation. . . . And He has committed to us the message of reconciliation. We are therefore Christ's ambassadors, as though God were making His appeal through us.
> *2 Corinthians 5:17-20*

> You are the salt of the earth. . . . You are the light of the world . . . let your light shine before men, that they may see your good deeds and praise your Father in heaven.
> *Matthew 5:13-14, 16*

> You are a chosen people . . . a people belonging to God, that you may declare the praises of Him who called you out of darkness into His wonderful light.
> *1 Peter 2:9*

Pastor and author Stuart Briscoe once said, "God doesn't save or bless anyone solely for his own benefit." When He touches us, He expects us to leave our fingerprints on the inhabitants of our Nineveh. And if we do that, we'll certainly break out of the penitentiary of boredom.

Whenever God calls you to a particular task, slip on your spiritual tennis shoes and go quickly. No matter what difficulties you face in the will of God, it beats a mouthful of salt water and a slimy bunk inside a fish's belly.

TURNING FEAR INTO FAITH

2 Chronicles 17:1–20:3

Tomorrow it's Ginny's turn to give a speech. She finds it hard enough to speak up during informal conversations—much less make a formal speech in front of peers when a grade is on the line. Her stomach feels like an ulcer factory. The thought of standing in front of that classroom paralyzes her.

Schoolwork weighs heavily on Greg's mind too. "I've got to raise my grades my senior year," he insists, "or I'll never get into a pre-med program. I've never wanted to be anything but a doctor. Besides, that's what my parents expect of me. Dad's counting on me going to his alma mater."

Bob, a rising high school junior, came home from summer camp to find a realty sign on his front lawn. His dad has been transferred out of state. They're shooting for a quick sale so the family can be settled again by the time school starts.

"I *hate* that realty sign!" Bob confided to his youth director. "For the first time in my life I have a couple of close pals, and I've been dating someone for a few months. I don't want to move and change schools or churches. Nobody knows me where we're going. Why can't my folks consider my feelings before making decisions?"

Vicky's spirit is bleak for a different reason. There's tension between her folks. She hears them arguing late at night when they think she's asleep. Her dad rarely arrives home from work in time to eat dinner with the family. Each parent vies for Vicky's sympathy, criticizing the other in front of her. She feels like human taffy, pulled in opposite directions by two emotionally starved adults. "Will they get a divorce?" she wonders. "What will happen to my nine-year-old brother and me?"

Ginny, Greg, Bob, and Vicky are toe-to-toe with a common enemy: *fear*. Fear is a common internal reaction to external challenges. We may not want to admit it, but the clammy fingers of fear grip all of us at one time or another. Whether it takes the form of anxiety over a public performance, insecurity over change, or worry over rejection, fear is a gut-wrenching emotion.

FRIEND OR FOE?

Before we go any further, let me emphasize that not all fear is bad. It's wise to be afraid of running across a busy highway with your eyes closed. And fear of the harmful consequences of breaking God's commands is a valid motivation for obedience. But when fear becomes a habitual response to life's challenges—when it saps our energy, injects pessimism into our attitudes, and keeps us from venturing into new activities or social relationships—we've got to label it an enemy. This unhealthy kind of fear is better described as *dread*, or *intimidation*. It puts a roadblock between us and our potential. Unless we conquer it, it leaves an emotional limp that will slow us down all our lives.

Be encouraged, though. If fear weighs you down, you *can* break its yoke. If you're a Christian, you have the resources of an all-powerful God at your disposal. He wants to turn your fear into faith. The process isn't easy—but it *is* possible.

What's involved in the process of transforming fear into faith? How can we tap into God's resources and develop strength to square off against peace-robbing situations? Is all the work up to God, or do we have responsibilities along the way?

To answer those questions, let's step back into the time tunnel once again and visit the kingdom of Judah. Turn the knob back to the ninth century before Christ's birth and look at King Jehoshaphat. When you read his story, you realize that the Bible is as up-to-date as the latest issue of *Seventeen* or *Newsweek*. Though we don't know what it's like to be a king, we can learn from Jehoshaphat how to cope with our own insecurities.

ROYAL REFORM

Second Chronicles 17–20 is like a slide show of Jehoshaphat's 25-year reign. Right from the first frame, we see his reliance on God:

> The Lord was with Jehoshaphat because in his early years he walked in the ways his father David had followed. He did not consult the Baals but sought the God of his father and followed His commands.
> . . . The Lord established the kingdom under his control; and all Judah brought gifts to Jehoshaphat, so that he had

> great wealth and honor. His heart was
> devoted to the ways of the Lord; further-
> more, he removed the high places and the
> Asherah poles from Judah. In the third
> year of his reign he sent his officials
> . . . to teach in the towns of Judah. They
> taught throughout Judah, taking with
> them the Book of the Law of the Lord.
> *2 Chronicles 17:3-7, 9*

Get the picture? He worked feverishly to stamp
out idolatry. (Baal and Asherah were man-made
gods. "High places" were altars built for offering
sacrifices to these false gods.) Then he mobilized a
team of itinerant Old Testament scholars to instruct
the people in correct ways of living and worshiping.

The results of Jehoshaphat's dedication to the
Lord took tangible form. Over a million young men
signed up for military duty. "The fear of the Lord fell
on all the kingdoms of the lands surrounding Judah,
so that they did not make war with Jehoshaphat.
Jehoshaphat became more and more powerful"
(17:10, 12).

So far, Jehoshaphat is the object of fear, not its
victim. But even for the noblest of people, the road
to maturity is dotted with chuckholes. Just when the
ride on his Michelins seemed smoothest, Jehoshaphat
made a wrong turn that temporarily knocked him out
of spiritual alignment.

A LOSING TEAM

Decades before Jehoshaphat moved to the
White House in Judah, the Jews experienced internal strife that literally split the nation in half. Two

countries emerged: Israel to the north, and Judah to the south. Each country boasted its own king. During Jehoshaphat's term in office, Ahab ruled Israel. The very name "Ahab" made godly people cringe. In stark contrast to Jehoshaphat, Ahab would easily be cast for a bad guy role on "The A-Team."

A foreign power, Ramoth Gilead, was threatening Israel's national security. Ahab devised a plan to improve his chances of winning a battle against this army. He pleaded with Jehoshaphat to join forces with Israel and attack the foreigners. It was a "let's-get-them-before-they-get-us" scheme.

At first, Jehoshaphat balked. He wanted to know if God would support the idea. Ahab paraded 400 false prophets—yes-men who didn't want to ignite Ahab's hot temper—who predicted victory in the battle. Sensing that these prophets had not heard from the true God, Jehoshaphat asked, "Is there not a prophet of the Lord here whom we can inquire of?" (18:6)

Reluctantly, Ahab summoned Micaiah. "I hate him," Ahab protested, "because he never prophesies anything good about me, but always bad" (18:7). Micaiah was more concerned about truth than popularity. He called the other prophets liars, and predicted disaster if the kings followed through with battle plans. Ahab, also true to form, tossed Micaiah into prison and put him on a diet of bread and water.

Did Jehoshaphat heed the warning and take the first chariot back to Judah? No. He bowed to Ahab's pressure and cooperated in the military venture.

The price of disobedience was high. Ramoth Gilead routed the Jewish forces, killing Ahab in the skirmish. Enemy chariots also singled out Jehoshaphat for attack, but he "cried out, and the Lord helped him" (18:31). He escaped to the peaceful confines of

Micaiah after Ahab is killed in
battle.

the well-fortified palace back in Jerusalem.

After Jehoshaphat returned to Judah, a spiritual adviser rebuked him for the alliance with Ahab. Jehu's words pricked the king's conscience: "Should you help the wicked and love those who hate the Lord? Because of this, the wrath of the Lord is upon you. There is, however, some good in you, for you rid the land of the Asherah poles and set your heart on seeking God" (19:2-3).

A good man had made a mistake. But he didn't make disobedience a habit. Jehoshaphat escalated efforts to reform Judah spiritually, and he appointed judges and priests to settle disputes among the people and administer the law of the Lord.

But even a good man's sin spawns negative consequences. Fallout from his alliance with Ahab was beginning to pollute the atmosphere in Judah. Neighboring countries that had been scared stiff of Jehoshaphat's army—and the obvious role God played in his success—now considered Judah more vulnerable.

"After all," his enemies might have mused, "his God didn't help him when he teamed with Ahab. Maybe his God has abandoned him. And the morale of their army is probably at an all-time low."

With such thoughts spurring them on, three foes of Jehoshaphat joined forces and marched toward Judah's border. "The Moabites and Ammonites with some of the Meunites came to make war on Jehoshaphat" (20:1). Their invasion spelled trouble—with a capital "T." The number of soldiers at Jehoshaphat's disposal paled compared to the invaders. Now the tables were turned. Fear grabbed Jehoshaphat by the throat and squeezed relentlessly.

Did Jehoshaphat wave a white flag and sign a declaration of surrender? If not, how did he break the stranglehold of fear?

CALL FOR HELP

His response gives us fear-fighting principle #1: *Admit your fear to the Lord.* "Jehoshaphat was afraid and turned his attention to seek the Lord, and proclaimed a fast throughout all Judah" (20:3, NASB). He told the Lord, "We . . . will cry out to You in our distress. . . . We have no power to face this vast army that is attacking us" (20:9, 12).

For Jehoshaphat, honest praying was a release valve for the pressure. He realistically appraised the situation, then hung a "Do Not Disturb" sign on the doorknob of his prayer closet. He didn't give God a snow job, nor pretend to have it all together. Instead of fiddling around, he yelled, "Help!"

May his tribe increase! God welcomes gut-level cries of that sort. Somebody has duped us into thinking that it isn't spiritual to confess weakness or inadequacy. Nonsense! God already knows we're inadequate. He's waiting for us to admit we can't handle things on our own. That's what frees Him to do a remodeling job with our lives. One of the best indicators of true spirituality is a willingness to cling to the Lord when burdens overwhelm us. Trying to conceal feelings of inadequacy is spiritual deceit.

God goes to great lengths to encourage us to bring our fears to Him. David wrote, "Cast your cares on the Lord and He will sustain you" (Psalm 55:22). Peter echoed that sentiment: "Cast all your anxiety on Him because He cares for you" (1 Peter 5:7). Would God command us to admit our fears if it were a subspiritual response to a crisis?

When we face our fears through prayer, God sometimes uses His power to reverse the threatening circumstance. But more often, He reverses our inner state and enables us to cope with the situation. He turns self-reliance into a humble dependence on

Him. He changes our perspective so we can view the situation as an opportunity to grow, rather than an enemy to avoid. He's more interested in changing *people* than things.

Some folks mock the habit of running to God with our fears. They think it's just an avenue of escape for wobbly kneed people. But when you break your leg, you're happy to have a crutch. In the same way, God is the support that each of us needs; leaning on Him gives us the strength to cope with life. It's nothing to be ashamed of—it's just a spiritual fact of life that all people need God.

Admitting you're afraid gets you off on the right foot. Yet the source of your fear is still blocking the path to spiritual victory. Clearing the path requires application of other fear-bumping insights found in 2 Chronicles 20.

Next we'll focus on the actual words in Jehoshaphat's prayers for help, and see how events unfolded afterward. You'll identify helpful attitudes that went hand in glove with Jehoshaphat's honesty. And you'll read about one of the most unusual military strategies ever implemented on the battlefield.

WHAT A DIFFERENCE A DAY MAKES

2 Chronicles 20:3-30

Every day of your life contains 24 hours—that's 1,440 minutes or 86,400 seconds. A lot happens in that span of time. In his trivia book titled *In One Day* (Houghton Mifflin), Tom Parker describes some things Americans do during an average day. Perhaps *you're* one of the leading contributors to these statistics.

In one day . . .

• Half a million Americans visit amusement parks—33 limp home with injuries.

• Americans drink enough soda pop to fill a bottle 530 feet tall. That amounts to 23 million gallons!

• We snap 21 million photographs (probably while sipping soft drinks and elbowing our way through amusement parks). That's more than 29 acres of wallet-size photos. If you worked at it 10 hours a day, it would take you *two years* to flip through them all in photo albums.

• Americans purchase at least 5 million items that are either shaped like Mickey Mouse or have a picture of Mickey Mouse on them.

● We eat 228,000 bushels of onions! (I don't have any statistics on the purchase of breath mints or toothpaste.)

● A whopping 25,000 Americans discover they have lice. (One surefire remedy is to breathe on them after eating all those onions.)

● Hamburger-hungry customers at McDonald's restaurants gulp down the equivalent of 2,250 head of cattle.

● Dogs—who aren't welcome at McDonald's—bite 20 mail carriers every day in America. The Postal Service dishes out $3,500 a day on medical expenses to treat the victims.

● Americans buy 4 million eraser-tipped pencils. That will erase all the mistakes from 1,500 miles of 8½″ by 11″ notebook paper—about 129 acres of goofs.

ONE LOUSY DAY

Back in chapter 8, we left Jehoshaphat stuck in a day that was far from typical. Believe me, the last thing on his mind was a Mickey Mouse souvenir, a chilled soda pop, or a McDonald's burger. In fact, he would gladly have traded his circumstances for a head full of lice *and* all 20 of those dog bites!

Three invading armies were perched on the border, eager to stamp out Jehoshaphat's soldiers and file a claim on Judah's property. Webster (of TV sitcom fame) would stand a better chance against Mr. T than Judah had against the invader. Jehoshaphat was no android—he was scared stiff. But he modeled the ideal response to threatening circumstances. He talked his fears over with the Lord.

No one could have predicted the scenario that developed over the next 24 hours. I don't know how many soda pops and Big Macs Jehoshaphat's army had, nor how many of their swords were branded with Mickey Mouse emblems. But I do know that it was one of the most eventful days in the nation's turbulent history. Let's watch the day unfold, and see what other fear-reducing principles crop up. You'll discover the origin of the cliché, "What a difference a day makes." Take my word for it— reading the next few pages won't rate as "trivial pursuit" for you.

Let's review fear-punching principle #1: *Admit your fear to the Lord, and plead for divine reinforcements.* Jehoshaphat knew he was in trouble and called for help. The next couple of points stem from the actual words in Jehoshaphat's prayer.

DIVINE PORTRAIT

Fear-fighting principle #2 grows out of the prayer Jehoshaphat flung toward heaven during a public assembly at the temple in Jerusalem:

> O Lord, God of our fathers, are You not the God who is in heaven? You rule over all the kingdoms of the nations. Power and might are in Your hand, and no one can withstand You.
> *2 Chronicles 20:6*

After admitting his fears, Jehoshaphat shifted his attention away from the threatening circumstance to a character portrait of God. Put simply, before fear can turn into faith, *we must mentally zero in on the qualities of our God.* Mulling over specific traits of our Lord stabilizes us. It reminds us that He's capable of either transforming our situation *or* transforming us so we can handle it.

Get a load of the divine attributes tucked away in that verse. Jehoshaphat shines the spotlight on God's *authority* over events. Nothing happens to us that surprises Him or foils His plans for our lives. Then he highlights God's *power* to intervene in the situation.

The next time fear gnaws at your soul, meditate on the features of God's character. What practical difference should it make to know that God is *wise?* That He never acts contrary to His *love* for you? Identifying characteristics of that sort serves as a catalyst for an inward change in attitude.

Fear turns to faith only when we have confidence in the Lord's ultimate mastery over the situation. To put it another way, what we genuinely *believe* about God affects our *attitudes* and *actions*. To know what we believe about God, we need to work at knowing God Himself. (For a close-up look at the Bible's portrait of God, get a copy of J.I. Packer's *Knowing God* [InterVarsity Press]. It's chock-full of substance, not fluff. Sifting through it trims the fat off lazy and shallow thinking about God.)

The longer you examine His portrait, the easier it will be to echo the psalmist's declaration: "God is our refuge and strength, an ever present help in trouble. Therefore we will not fear, though the earth give way and the mountains fall into the heart of the sea" (Psalm 46:1-2).

PAST PERFORMANCE

Not only did Jehoshaphat pinpoint characteristics of God, but he also beamed his thoughts to past actions of God on behalf of the nation. He prayed:

> O our God, did You not drive out the
> inhabitants of this land before Your peo-
> ple Israel and give it forever to the de-
> scendants of Abraham Your friend?
> *2 Chronicles 20:7*

Jehoshaphat retrieved memories stored in his
mental data bank. Centuries earlier, God had promised Abraham that his descendants—composed of the
divided kingdoms of Israel and Judah—would inherit
a prime piece of real estate. God miraculously deliv-
ered the Jews from slavery in Egypt. Then He
helped them ransack pagan inhabitants of Canaan
and stake a claim on the land. Jehoshaphat recalled
God's past provision of the land he occupied—which
was now threatened with a foreign invasion.

You can bank on it: noting specific evidences of
God's past involvement bolstered Jehoshaphat's
faith.

Let's reduce this third fear-smashing insight to a
sentence: When fear is hot on your trail, *remember
how the Lord has come through for you in the past.*
When you recall past instances of His faithfulness, it
becomes a bit easier to trust Him in the current
threatening situation.

In *Stand Tough*, a SonPower book about ways to
keep your faith in rough circumstances, I illustrated
how one girl applied this principle:

> One girl I know helps remember her past
> with God by keeping a prayer journal.
> She jots down her requests, the date she
> begins to pray, how God answers, and the
> date of each answer.
>
> She says, "I don't always get the an-
> swers I hoped for, but I've been surprised

at how often I've seen God working in my life. Even when He answers with a no, I'm discovering His faithfulness. Looking back, I can see that some of the things I've asked for wouldn't have been good for me. When I'm discouraged, it's a big help to flip through my journal and remember God's goodness. (p. 127)

Before reading any further, take several minutes to flip through *your* mental scrapbook. What memories of God's involvement leap off the pages? How did He answer prayers that you offered under pressure? From the perspective of time, how have you grown spiritually as a result of standing neck deep in threatening circumstances?

I call this type of mental excursion "putting the past into present tense." It's saying to God, "I don't understand nor like what's happening right now. But I see too many past examples of Your faithfulness to stop trusting You."

From Jehoshaphat's example, we've identified three things to do when fear hounds us:

● Admit you're afraid. Dial the Lord's 911 number and request emergency reinforcements.

● Concentrate on the Lord's character traits, and mull over their practical applications to your fear-producing circumstance.

● Identify ways He has come through for you in the past.

Those aren't the only insights from 2 Chronicles 20 that can keep us from throwing in the towel, though. When Jehoshaphat finished his prayer during the mass meeting in front of the temple, something happened that wasn't on the agenda. Let's pick up the story:

All the men of Judah, with their wives
and children and little ones, stood there
before the Lord.

Then the Spirit of the Lord came upon
Jahaziel . . . as he stood in the assembly.

He said: "Listen, King Jehoshaphat and
all who live in Judah and Jerusalem! This
is what the Lord says to you: 'Do not be
afraid or discouraged because of this vast
army. For the battle is not yours, but
God's. Tomorrow march down against
them. They will be climbing up by the
Pass of Ziz, and you will find them at the
end of the gorge in the Desert of Jeruel.
You will not have to fight this battle.
Take up your positions; stand firm and
see the deliverance the Lord will give
you, O Judah and Jerusalem. Do not be
afraid; do not be discouraged. Go out to
face them tomorrow, and the Lord will be
with you.' "

2 Chronicles 20:13-17

Chances are, this prophet raised a few eyebrows
when he said, "You will not have to fight this battle."
What did he mean? Could Judah defeat three armies
without lifting a finger?

Whoa. . . . Let's preserve the climax for later. Before discovering what God had up His sleeve, let's
acknowledge a fourth fear-crushing truth: *The perspective or encouragement of another believer can
carry us through rough times.* God had miraculously
revealed His plans to Jahaziel 24 hours in advance.
He verbally inflated the sagging confidence of the
people by informing them that God would intervene.

Now that we have the Bible, God normally doesn't

reveal such classified information to individuals. All that we need to know to live out our faith from day to day is already provided in the 66 books of His written Word. But that fact doesn't diminish the importance of the principle. God still strengthens us and communicates to us at timely moments through the counsel of other Christians.

No one is expected to make it alone as a believer. God knows that living for Him, sharing our faith with non-Christians, and working out our problems are tasks far beyond our own ability. So He has provided help—Christians who relate closely to one another and help each other along. I build my case with verses like Proverbs 17:17: "A friend loves at all times, and a brother is born for adversity." Or Galatians 6:2: "Carry each other's burdens."

Fear drains the energy out of our emotional batteries. That's when we need an encourager to replenish our supply and restore our hope. In an article titled "The Encouragement Connection" in *New Covenant* magazine, Virgil Vogt compares an encourager to a jumper cable:

> The New Testament Greek word for encouragement contains the idea of being called alongside another. On the coldest winter days we do this to some of our cars. They need encouragement! When one battery is so weak that it cannot spark its engine, we bring another car alongside and connect the working battery with heavy jumper cables to the weaker battery. Nothing is changed in the car that won't start. But with the direct infusion of power from the other vehicle, the weakness is overcome and

the stranded car is able to function on its own. We Christians often need to connect with the strength in others in order to get started or to keep going in difficult circumstances. We need someone to come alongside and give us a jump.

The next time you're running shy on courage and faith, consult a close friend or an adult you can trust. Ask that person to pray for you and to share any counsel that could shed light on your dark situation. Don't keep to yourself because you're afraid that person will view you as a spiritual toddler. If you choose a mature person, he or she will commend you for being so transparent. No one can give you a "jump" until you're willing to raise the hood and admit that your battery is low.

Sometimes private prayer provides all the boost we need. Yet on other occasions we need "God with skin on." The objective input of a vibrant Christian is often the key that unlocks our lives and releases pent-up fears and anxieties. God has opted to speak to us through other people who know His Word.

Because he reaped the benefits of the four principles we've described, Jehoshaphat's faith ascended to higher elevations. But he wasn't to the top yet. There were still three armies to contend with. Humanly speaking, the battle still had all the makings of a *Guinness Book of World Records* slaughter—in favor of the enemy!

UNEXPECTED STRATEGY
The story resumes at sunrise the next morning. Judah's troops are ready to march out to the desert and confront the invaders.

As they set out, Jehoshaphat stood and
said, "Listen to me, Judah and people of
Jerusalem! Have faith in the Lord your
God and you will be upheld. . . . " Jehoshaphat appointed men to sing to the Lord
and to praise Him for the splendor of His
holiness as they went out at the head of
the army, saying:
"Give thanks to the Lord,
for His love endures forever."
2 Chronicles 20:20-21

What Jehoshaphat did probably caused his drill ser-
geants to break out in a rash. To say the least, it was
an unconventional military strategy. In front of the
procession of combat soldiers he placed musicians
and singers. When he gave the signal to march, the
Jerusalem Tabernacle Choir led the caravan with
songs of praise to God.

That's the lineup you'd expect if they were return-
ing to the city *after* a resounding victory—not how
you'd proceed *before* squaring off against the enemy.
The procession demonstrated Jehoshaphat's confidence in God. He regarded victory as so certain that
he acted as if it were already a fact. And God re-
warded his faith.

As they began to sing and praise, the
Lord set ambushes against the
men . . . who were invading Judah, and
they were defeated. . . . When the men
of Judah came to the place that overlooks
the desert and looked toward the vast
army, they saw only dead bodies lying on
the ground; no one had escaped. So Je-

Jehoshaphat's army arrives at the battle site.

hoshaphat and his men went to carry off
their plunder, and they found among
them a great amount of equipment and
clothing and also articles of value—more
than they could take away. . . .

Then, led by Jehoshaphat, all the men
of Judah and Jerusalem returned joyfully
to Jerusalem. . . .

The fear of God came upon all the kingdoms of the countries when they heard
how the Lord had fought against the enemies of Israel. And the kingdom of Jehoshaphat was at peace, for his God had
given him rest on every side.

2 Chronicles 20:22-30

Did the Lord send extraterrestrial beings to am-
bush the three invading armies? No. Two of the
armies ganged up on the third. After they annihi-
lated the outnumbered regime, the two victors
knocked off each other. God miraculously intervened
by causing jealousies and feuds to erupt, prompting
edgy troops to draw the sword against others in the
same camp. By the time Judah's recruits arrived,
there was no one left to fight.

From those climactic events emerges this final
fear-erasing principle: *Praising God when we're under the whip of trying circumstances stabilizes our
trust in Him.*

Did you notice that they began praising God
before He routed their foes? They had admitted
their fears . . . reflected on God's character . . . recalled His past performances on their behalf . . . and
received the encouragement of someone who had
a hot line to God. That process enabled them to

worship God even before their problem was resolved. Praise increases faith because it shifts our thoughts away from ourselves and beams them toward God. Such a radical shift in focus releases God's power in our lives.

I'd be less than honest, though, if I didn't admit one gut-ripping fact of the Christian life. You'll face times when God chooses *not* to demolish the threats to your sanity. He won't always intervene externally. But even then, He'll want to intervene *internally* and slaughter any fears that oppress you. That's because His consuming interest is in having a *relationship* with you. And nothing can deepen your intimacy with Him or your trust in Him like a few problems now and then. Most of us don't edge closer to God unless we *have* to!

Besides, turning your fear into faith is a greater miracle than removing the source of your fear. In Jehoshaphat's case, that fear-into-faith process took only one day. It may take longer for you, but God can do it. For He's more interested in your *transformation* than He is in your making the *In One Day* trivia book.

HOW DO YOU SPELL "RELIEF"?

Mark 5:1-20

When a problem baffles you. . . .

When an unanswered question has you in a hammerlock. . . .

When an unmet need burns a softball-size hole in your mind. . . .

When you're long on confusion and short on wisdom. . . .

Then you need an expert. According to Webster, an "expert" is someone with special knowledge, skill, or experience who comes to the rescue of folks like you and me who have less on the ball. If we'd appeal to such authority figures more often, we'd have fewer hassles.

This is one area in which we can learn a lot from young kids. They don't hesitate to approach experts with their dilemmas.

As a case in point, look over the following letters they wrote to veterinarians (compiled by Bill Adler). When pet problems surfaced, they didn't beat around the bush. They consulted men and women in the know.

Dear Dr. Smith:
Is popcorn good for dogs? I hope so—my dog, Aggie, just ate a whole box.
Howard

Dear Pet Doctor:
Are dogs supposed to be smarter than people? My dog is smarter than my big brother.
Billy

Dear Pet Doctor:
I like my pet cat a lot. She isn't afraid of anything except my father, but that isn't really surprising, because everybody is afraid of him.
Wendy

Dear Dr. Holden:
My grandma got me a turtle for my birthday. Are turtles good for anything other than creeping around?
Amy

Dear Dr. Holmes:
I bought a hamster at the pet store. My mother screamed when she saw him. Is something wrong with my hamster—or my mother?
Dennis

I'm not minimizing unresolved pet problems. But for the majority of life's desperate situations, we need someone whose expertise is far broader than turtles and tomcats. We need the intervention of someone who boasts blameless credentials on life management.

You guessed it—the ultimate expert on life is Jesus Christ. And He's approachable 24 hours a day, seven days a week. In this chapter and the next, you'll meet three first-century characters who shared one thing in common: they were pestered by predicaments too hard for them to handle. They desperately needed expert help, and each of them spelled "relief" J-E-S-U-S.

Chapter 5 of Mark's Gospel narrates the stories of these people, whom you'll meet in chapters 10 and 11. Lots of practical truths leapfrog off the pages, so catch as many as you can. But hammer one basic point deep into your consciousness: the same divine expertise that Jesus demonstrates in these episodes is available to you as well.

WELCOME TO MY TOMB

The first stop on our journey through Mark 5 is alongside the Sea of Galilee in ancient Palestine. It's rather early in Jesus' earthly ministry. He has been roaming from place to place, teaching about the kingdom of God and performing occasional miracles. Moments before the scene opens, Jesus accomplished a head-turning feat that made the network news broadcast back in Jerusalem: He instantaneously calmed a boat-rocking thunderstorm while sailing with His disciples across the sea (Mark 4:35-41). Now He's getting out of the boat, with the 12 disciples tagging along behind, caboose-style. Before they can find a McDonald's or a Ramada Inn, a stranger bolts across the beach and confronts Jesus. Let's pick up the action in verse 2:

> When Jesus got out of the boat, a man with an evil spirit came from the tombs to

meet Him. This man lived in the tombs, and no one could bind him anymore, not even with a chain. For he had often been chained hand and foot, but he tore the chains apart and broke the irons on his feet. No one was strong enough to subdue him. Night and day among the tombs and in the hills he would cry out and cut himself with stones.

When he saw Jesus from a distance, he ran and fell on his knees in front of Him. He shouted at the top of his voice, "What do you want with me, Jesus, Son of the Most High God? Swear to God that You won't torture me!" For Jesus was saying to him, "Come out of this man, you evil spirit!"

Then Jesus asked him, "What is your name?"

"My name is Legion," he replied, "for we are many." And he begged Jesus again and again not to send them out of the area.

Mark 5:2-10

Here's one of several demon-possessed individuals mentioned in the four Gospels (Matthew, Mark, Luke, and John). We don't want to get stuck in theological quicksand, but let's review notes from a New Testament 101 course on Satan and demons.

PRINCES OF DARKNESS

Demons are Satan's agents who operate in the sphere of time and space. These spiritual beings are hostile to both God and man. The Apostle

Paul warned Christians about the army of invisible spiritual forces whom Satan masterminds.

> Put on all of God's armor so that you will be able to stand safe against all strategies and tricks of Satan. For we are not fighting against people made of flesh and blood, but against persons without bodies—the evil rulers of the unseen world, those mighty satanic beings and great evil princes of darkness who rule this world; and against huge numbers of wicked spirits in the spirit world.
> *Ephesians 6:11-12*, TLB

There is no question that demons exist and that their activities are very real. The demon-possessed man that Jesus met certainly knew the reality and torment of demonic activity.

In this instance, a mob of demons controlled the man's mind and emotions. That explains the collective name "Legion." They actually took over his vocal cords and spoke for him. Their reign in his life was short-lived, though. Jesus staged a military coup and expelled the demons from the man, casting them into a herd of 2,000 pigs. The swine dashed into the lake and were drowned. Residents of the area, furious over the loss of all that ham and pork roast, begged Jesus to leave their region.

Jesus demonstrated unsurpassed expertise in handling supernatural evil. (The trio from *Ghostbusters* pale in comparison to His devil-defeating power!) No longer did self-destructive behavior plague the man. Luke's version of this story vividly shows the before-and-after contrast: "They found the man from whom the demons had gone out, sitting at Jesus' feet, dressed and in his right mind" (Luke 8:35).

He pleaded to go with Jesus, but the Lord had a better plan:

> Jesus did not let him, but said, "Go home to your family and tell them how much the Lord has done for you, and how He has had mercy on you." So the man went away and began to tell . . . how much Jesus had done for him. And all the people were amazed.
>
> *Mark 5:19-20*

Look closely, and in every historical event recorded in Scripture you'll notice one or more truths that apply to daily experience. What is God saying through the story line you just skimmed? I find three insights valuable enough to deposit in your mind's vault.

SUPERNATURAL TERRORISM

Satan is a real force to be reckoned with. No one who respects the Bible can scoff at him and pass him off as some medieval myth or imaginary boogeyman. Jesus' tussel with the demons should prick us with the reality of spiritual warfare. We have an adversary so fiendish that by comparison, Lex Luther comes across as the best man at Superman's wedding. Satan pulls out all the stops to drag us down spiritually. No terrorist can match his appetite for destruction. That's why Peter told his readers, "Be self-controlled and alert. Your enemy the devil prowls around like a roaring lion looking for someone to devour" (1 Peter 5:8). In *Living with Your Passions* (Victor Books), Erwin Lutzer says,

"Though Satan cannot possess Christians (possession implies an ownership that belongs to God alone), he can invade a life, particularly if we have opened the door to evil influences" (p. 135).

If you think satanic activity was just a first-century phenomenon, get a load of the following facts:

● The occult movement boasts its own trade magazine, *Occult Trade Journal.* In the 1970s, when Doubleday publishers opened a new book club of occult titles, membership zoomed to 100,000 in two years.

● San Francisco has a church of Satan, nestled in a middle-class neighborhood. The church shows interested outsiders a film called *Satanist,* which unveils the church's rituals: black-robed men and women conducting a black mass with a nude woman on the altar. Members proudly proclaim their hate and lust. The leader, Anton LaVey, blesses them, saying, "May all your lustful thoughts reach fruition. Hail Satan!" The church claims 7,000 fee-paying members.

● Satan worshipers broke into several churches in Oakland Park, Florida and performed what police termed "sexual black masses." Following the sex rituals, participants wrecked furniture and smashed liturgical objects. In one of the churches, the guest book was signed "Satan."

● In Norman, Oklahoma, members of a secret teenage fraternity professing devotion to Satan were blamed for four incidents of vandalism over a nine-month period. The fraternity adopted the name "Covenant of the 73rd Demon." Members vandalized church property—ripping Bibles apart, turning crosses upside down, etc.—to prove their loyalty to the devil (Paul Lee Tan, *Encyclopedia of 7,700*

Illustrations, Assurance Publishers, pp. 911, 919, 920).

But the presence of God's Spirit tips the scales in the Christian's favor. "Greater is He who is in you than he who is in the world" (1 John 4:4, NASB). Yet if we take our rival for granted, we make a fatal mistake. Overcoming Satan's temptations requires active participation on our part. We must choose to use the weapons of spiritual warfare that the Lord has provided: prayer, Bible study, and fellowship with other Christians. The moment our spiritual muscles become flabby or we let down our defenses, he can sneak in a knockout punch.

There's a word for the person who doesn't work at resisting the devil: *victim*.

BELIEF ISN'T ENOUGH

Nodding in agreement with Bible truths doesn't make anyone a Christian. One of the first persons to correctly identify Jesus as the Son of God was a demon, using the vocal cords of a man. Before Jesus expelled him, the demon bellowed, "I know who You are—the Holy One of God!" (Mark 1:24) Before the exorcism, the demon-possessed man you just read about acknowledged the same truth: "What do You want with me, Jesus, Son of the Most High God?" (Mark 5:7)

A couple decades later, James tried to convince his readers that mere agreement with right doctrine didn't reserve them an executive suite in heaven. "You believe that there is one God," he wrote. "Good! Even the demons believe that—and shudder" (James 2:19).

Imagine . . . the devil could pass a theology exam! Don't skirt this issue. Entering a relationship with

"You believe that there is one God. Good! Even the demons believe that—and shudder" (James 2:19).

Christ involves a response of your *will*. He enters your life only when you extend a personal invitation. That invitation involves agreeing with Him that you've sinned and need a Saviour. It means making Him your Lord. It requires a change of mind about your lifestyle, being fed up with the status quo, willing to shuck any behavior pattern that displeases God.

Sure, the invitation assumes that you believe certain things about Jesus. But you'll find that lots of folks who hold correct opinions about Him won't know the password when they arrive at the Pearly Gates.

After all, you won't meet any demons in heaven. . . .

CHANGE AGENT

Witnessing is first and foremost a spontaneous overflow of a life that has been changed by Jesus. The restored demoniac darted back to his hometown and shared "how much Jesus had done for him" (Mark 5:20).

Victimized by his own antisocial outbursts, the man had lived like a hermit. Ugly, self-inflicted gashes covered his body. Not even a psychiatrist could get close enough for an interview. Yet one brush with Jesus caused his life to take a 180-degree turn. After that, he talked about Jesus not because he felt he *ought* to, but because he *wanted* to.

When you're wondering what to say to non-Christians, remember Jesus' words to the man: "Tell them how much the Lord has done for you, and how He has had mercy on you" (5:19).

Imagine that He's firing that command at you right now. What specific data about God's work in your life come to mind? That's what you share! Talk about the capacity He has given you to hold your temper around the house. Mention specific prayers He has answered, goals He has redirected, or a harmful relationship He enabled you to break off. Verbally give Jesus the credit for any before-and-after contrasts you can identify.

A witness is more than a slicked-up dude with the fastest Bible in town, who can shoot you down with Scripture from Genesis to Revelation. Sharing Christ is more than leaving a tract with your tip or pasting a "Honk if you love Jesus" bumper sticker on your car. More Bible knowledge and discreet use of printed materials can increase your effectiveness as a witness. But anyone whom Christ has changed is qualified to give a testimony. After all, that's what Jesus said to do—and He's the expert.

FAITH HAS
THE LAST LAUGH

Mark 5:21-43

———

Want to inject new vitality into your prayer life without increasing your self-discipline? Perhaps the "Godbox" is your answer. *Group* magazine disclosed the availability of this innovative device:

> For a direct line to heaven, the "Godbox" is your answer, claims A Creative Company, based in Carson City, Nevada.
>
> The Godbox is a small container made of leather-like material and gold-stamped. The Godbox is also available in wood with a lasered top. And buyers may personalize their Godboxes with their names gold-stamped on the product for an extra fee.
>
> "The box is designed to relay the owner's prayers directly to God's care," says Jerry Goossen, one of three stockholders of the Godbox company. "You simply write your problems or desires on a pre-printed prayer sheet, drop the prayer in the box, and let God take over," he ex-

plains. According to Goossen, users of the Godbox are pleased with the results. (*Group*, September 1984, p. A-16)

The basic Godbox sells for $14.95, and the simulated leather version is $29.95. With a lasered wood top a Godbox's price tag is $69.95. You can find it in gift, novelty, and religious stores nationwide. It comes with an unconditional money-back guarantee.

I'm not convinced that doling out cash for a "Godbox" will improve your prayer life. (*Group* magazine wasn't endorsing the product either.) The only surefire stimulant I know for consulting the Lord is *an impossible situation*. When all our strategies backfire and a sense of helplessness envelopes us, we're more apt to call on God—Godbox or no Godbox!

Mark 5 tells the stories of three people who were mired in the muck of hopeless situations. You've already met the man strapped with "Legionnaire's" disease (spiritually speaking). Jesus instantly came up with an antidote for his demon possession.

Now you'll encounter two other folks who needed a direct line to heaven. Along with other practical insights for living, their episodes offer answers to these questions:

● When you're in a tight spot, what kind of approach to the Lord pleases Him and gets results?

● What is there about Jesus Christ that should motivate us to approach Him more often with our needs?

Soak up the details of these slice-of-life anecdotes and you'll save at least $14.95.

LAST RESORT

The second stop on our expedition through Mark 5 is on the opposite side of the Sea of Galilee. Just a few grains of sand have passed through the hourglass since Jesus cured the demon-possessed man. As He steps out of the boat and starts sloshing to shore, a throng of curious autograph seekers huddle on the beach. They're agog with gossip about Jesus' latest exploit when a frantic stranger bulldozes his way through the crowd and flings himself at Jesus' feet.

Hysterically, he screams, "Please, Jesus—you've got to come with me! My 12-year-old girl is dying, and You're the only hope I have left. Hurry!"

The fearful father is Jairus, a respected ruler of the Jewish synagogue. Jesus elbows His way through the crowd and starts following the man. The road to Jairus' house, though, is strewn with detours, the most prominent one being another desperate human being. As you read about her intrusion into Jairus' plans, put yourself in the shoes of the apprehensive father. If you were Jairus, what would be going through your mind as you observed the event that unfolded next?

> A large crowd followed and pressed around Him. And a woman was there who had been subject to bleeding for twelve years. She had suffered a great deal under the care of many doctors and had spent all she had, yet instead of getting better, she grew worse. When she heard about Jesus, she came up behind Him in the crowd and touched His cloak, because she thought, "If I just touch His clothes, I will be healed." Immediately

her bleeding stopped and she felt in her body that she was freed from her suffering.

At once Jesus realized that power had gone out from Him. He turned around in the crowd and asked, "Who touched My clothes?"

"You see the people crowding against You," His disciples answered, "and yet You can ask, 'Who touched Me?'"

But Jesus kept looking around to see who had done it. Then the woman, knowing what had happened to her, came and fell at His feet and, trembling with fear, told Him the whole truth. He said to her, "Daughter, your faith has healed you. Go in peace and be freed from your suffering."

Mark 5:24-34

This woman had tried everything for her physical ailment, including 11 separate prescriptions that were listed in the *Talmud*. (The Jews lugged around this hefty hardback, consisting of commentary on and intricate application of the Law of Moses.) Then she drained her savings account on doctor calls and prescription drugs. When she had exhausted all other means of relief, rumors of Jesus' power reached her ears. One last ray of hope split the darkness in her heart. She got Jesus' attention and clung to Him like a crab until His power infused her body.

MEANWHILE...

How was Jairus handling the delay? If I'd been wearing his Florsheims, the whole incident

with the woman would've eaten away at me like acid.
My thoughts would progress along these lines: "She's
waited 12 years for a cure—surely a few more hours
won't make any difference. My girl can't afford to
wait. Take care of her first, Jesus; *then* give the
woman a page out of your Day-Timer."

I'm not sure if that's what Jairus was thinking, but
the interruption no doubt gave him the fidgets. And
for good reason. While Jesus was still chatting with
the woman, some messengers came from the house
of Jairus with this news: "Your daughter is dead,"
they reported. "Why bother the teacher any more?"
(5:35)

At that moment an emotionally numb Jairus felt so
low that he had to stand on tiptoe in order to touch
bottom. Then Jesus, shifting His attention once again
to Jairus, brushed aside the tragic news.

"Don't be afraid," He told Jairus, "just believe"
(5:36). Jairus had nothing to depend on except the
words of Jesus. With a lump in his throat and circumstances against his faith, he led Jesus to the house
where the girl's body lay. The verses that follow
provide the climax.

When they came to the home of the synagogue ruler, Jesus saw a commotion, with
people crying and wailing loudly. He went
in and said to them, "Why all this commotion and wailing? The child is not dead but
asleep." But they laughed at Him.

After He put them all out, He took the
child's father and mother and the disciples
who were with Him, and went in where
the child was. He took her by the hand
and said to her, *"Talitha koum!"* (which
means, "Little girl, I say to you, get

up!"). Immediately the girl stood up and
walked around (she was twelve years
old). At this they were completely
astonished.

Mark 5:38-42

Don't let Jesus' reference to the girl being asleep
throw you for a loop. The girl had definitely stopped
breathing. Jesus was saying that, for all practical
purposes, she might as well be asleep. It was as easy
for Him to rouse her from death as it was to awaken
her from sleep.

The mourners who laughed at Jesus wound up
with egg on their faces, but Jairus had the last laugh.
Funeral arrangements were canceled. The next day's
issue of the *Capernaum Chronicle* probably contained an ad saying, "FOR SALE: ONE TOMB.
NEVER USED."

Remember the demon-possessed man Jesus had
just left? Before squaring off against Jesus, he literally pitched his tent in a graveyard. He "lived in the
tombs" (5:3). Think of it . . . Mark 5 opens in a
graveyard and closes by avoiding one!

Once again, it's time to ask the most basic of all
Bible study questions: *so what?* Unapplied Bible
knowledge is dangerous stuff. As we investigate the
stories of Jairus and the woman, what life-related
principles stalk us?

FORUM ON FAITH

One theme woven throughout the fabric of
these episodes is *faith*. When push came to shove,
Jairus and the woman put their trust in Jesus. Here
are three faith-related truths that shout through a
megaphone for our attention.

● **1. Faith in Jesus reveals itself in action.**
What we believe about the Lord becomes *faith* when
we *act* upon something He has said, or take the
initiative to pray about a need. Both characters exerted teeth-gritting effort in order to find Jesus and
to drop their requests at His feet. No matter how
strongly they believed in Jesus' power, if they had
failed to track Him down, they wouldn't have experienced it.

It's the kind of faith that nudges us out of the
stands of formal religion and onto the playing field of
authentic Christianity. In *If God Loves Me, Why
Can't I Get My Locker Open?* (Bethany), Lorraine
Peterson adds a footnote to this point:

> If I really believe something strongly
> enough, I will act on it. If I'm convinced
> that understanding chemistry will help
> me get through nurses' training, I'll study
> hard. If I'm certain that I can't make the
> cheerleading squad, I won't even try out.
> If I really believe the ice will hold, I'll go
> snowmobiling on the frozen lake. Saying,
> "I believe the ice will hold, but I'd never
> walk out on it," would reveal my lack of
> faith.
>
> If you really believe in Jesus, you'll
> want to trust Him. There is an old story
> about a man who walked on a tightrope
> across Niagara Falls. Next, he wheeled
> an empty wheelbarrow across the rope
> above Niagara Falls. Then he asked his
> applauding crowd, "Do you believe that I
> can put a man in the wheelbarrow and
> still make it across?" Everyone shouted,
> "Yes!" Then he asked, "Who will get into

the wheelbarrow?" No one volunteered.
(p. 21)

Do *you* have "get-into-the-wheelbarrow" faith?
That's what it takes to break off a relationship which
is damaging you spiritually. You trust Jesus to fill
the vacuum this person leaves, to satisfy the inner
craving for companionship. "Wheelbarrow faith" is
needed when you're tempted to lash out at the
person who spread false rumors about you. Instead
of sinning in response to sin, you trust Jesus to
vindicate your character and punish the wrongdoer.
To exercise such faith requires confidence in the
Lord. Your faith is only as strong as its object.

● **2. Faith and fear can coexist.** Be encouraged.
Learning to trust was a process for Bible people too.
They weren't born with an extra gland that secreted
faith. The fact that Jairus pleaded so desperately
with Jesus—plus Jesus' words, "Don't be afraid"
(5:36)—shows that he had sweaty palms and a racing
heartbeat. Yet his coming to Jesus, and his willingness to lead Jesus to the house even after news of the
girl's death, also revealed faith.

If your faith wobbles a bit during rough times,
welcome to the human race. Don't feel shot down
because the height of your trust is sometimes below
sea level. Too often we get all out of sorts because we
put our faith in our faith rather than in a Person. Put
what little faith you have in Jesus. Tell Him you're
eager to enroll in His "Faith-Building 101" course.
You won't have to wait long for classes to begin.

● **3. God often tests and deepens faith through
times of delay.** How long had the woman been
handcuffed to a physical ailment? Twelve years. And
though Jairus' delay was measured in moments, to
wait as his daughter hovered near death was gut-

wrenching. Let's face it—sometimes we're in a hurry
and God isn't.

When is waiting the most frustrating for you?
When God answers your prayers with silence? When
you peer into an empty mailbox—*again?* When every prospective summer employer says, "I'll keep
your application on file"?

View delays of this sort from the crest of Mount
Perspective. God isn't toying with your emotions.
He's trying to whip you into shape, to lower the rate
of your spiritual heartbeat. And that requires work-
outs in the gymnasium of adversity. Here's how
James described this toughening-up process:

> Consider it pure joy, my brothers, when-
> ever you face trials of many kinds, be-
> cause you know that the testing of your
> faith develops perseverance. Persever-
> ance must finish its work so that you may
> be mature and complete, not lacking
> anything.
>
> *James 1:2-4*

The term translated "testing" means "proving." It
carries the idea of proving, or exposing, the quality
of our faith or character with the ultimate goal of
gaining a stamp of approval. Delay is a "test of faith"
because it *proves* beyond a shadow of a doubt where
we are spiritually. Waiting reveals whether our security is rooted in circumstances or in our relationship
with the Lord.

Even if we make a failing grade and react with a
complaining spirit, the quiz posed by delay has educational value. Before we can strengthen our faith,
we have to see its flabby condition in the mirror.
Only stark realization of our need will spur us to

enroll in an ongoing spiritual fitness program.

What follows are comments I've heard from young Christians who looked back on experiences of delay and saw spiritual benefits:

> When I'm forced to wait on God's next move, I tend to listen more attentively to what He's trying to say through the situation. Spiritually speaking, it's as if slowing down the pace improves my hearing.

> Going through delay gives the Holy Spirit an opportunity to put my motives through the third degree. Once, while waiting to hear about a job I applied for, He showed me that I wanted that position for all the wrong reasons. I confessed the impurity, and experienced that all-vacuumed-out-inside feeling that comes only when we let the Lord do house cleaning. Without the extra couple weeks of delay, I would've been too busy to hear the Holy Spirit's rebuke.

> When things don't fall into place for me—like when I'm waiting on someone else to make a decision that affects me—I pray a lot more. I guess anything that makes me pray is a blessing in disguise.

The next time God puts you on hold, listen attentively to the background music on the line. There's a message for you in it. V. Raymond Edman, the late president of Wheaton College, said: "Delay never thwarts God's purposes. It polishes His instruments."

God's school of character building.

THE RIGHT APPROACH

Long before someone conjured up the idea of a "Godbox," Jesus was responsive to the sincere approaches of folks in need. Besides their faith, what was there about Jairus and the woman that tapped the power of the Lord? When their faith was X-rayed under pressure, what did they model for us about approaching the Lord?

● **1. They approached Him boldly.** Both individuals shoved their way through a crowd to gain a hearing for their requests. Neither was bashful, hesitant, or apologetic about interrupting Jesus' schedule. Neither cared what onlookers thought about their public plea for help.

A couple decades after these encounters, Jesus' half brother James wrote, "You do not have, because you do not ask God" (James 4:2). Jairus and the woman wanted to make sure that if they missed a miracle, it wouldn't be because they failed to ask for one. Perhaps they got wind of comments publicly made by Jesus himself, in which He discouraged hesitancy about approaching Him with needs. Jesus once said, "Come to Me, all you who are weary and burdened, and I will give you rest" (Matthew 11:28).

Someone once told me that he didn't pray boldly because he didn't feel worthy enough to approach a holy God. Whether his need was a nagging circumstance or a sin he wanted to confess, he'd shrink from praying because He didn't think God would accept him.

I reminded him that no one is ever acceptable to God on the basis of his or her own performance. Our *only* basis for acceptance by God, and our only right to approach Him boldly with our needs, is grounded in our relationship with Jesus Christ. We tag "in Jesus' name" onto the ends of our prayers because it says that Jesus' death on the cross gives us the right to enter God's presence. Our Heavenly Father accepts you and me on the basis of *Jesus'* perfection— never our own behavioral report card.

Satan tries to short-circuit our prayer lives by making us feel too inferior to approach God. He shifts the focus away from the benefits of Jesus' death, to our own frailties. When those feelings surface, we can fight him with the truth of Hebrews 4:14-16:

> Jesus the Son of God is our great High Priest who has gone to heaven itself to help us; therefore let us never stop trusting Him. This High Priest of ours understands our weaknesses, since He had the same temptations we do, though He never once gave way to them and sinned. So let us come *boldly* to the very throne of God and stay there to receive His mercy and to find grace to help us in our times of need.
>
> *Hebrews 4:14-16, TLB (italics added)*

● **2. Jairus and the woman approached Jesus humbly.** When Jairus spotted Jesus, "he *fell at His feet* and pleaded earnestly with Him" (Mark 5:22-23). A few seconds after she touched Jesus' cloak and experienced instantaneous healing, the woman "came and *fell at His feet*" (5:33).

Their earth-hugging posture reflected a submissive spirit. Though they flung their needs at Him boldly, they weren't arrogant. They understood that their purity and power were no match for His. That's humility—the ability to see the striking difference between you and God. A person who has a realistic view of himself can't help but feel humble. One who has a correct view of the Lord can't, by comparison, ever feel proud.

A proud approach to God subtly communicates this message: "God, I haven't committed any gross sins in recent weeks. And the last time I prayed things didn't pan out the way I wanted. I feel like You owe me this one."

A humble approach says, "Father, I deserve none of Your benefits. When I think of Your holiness and my sinfulness, I'm reminded that the only reason I can approach You with this request is because Jesus paid for my sins. I'm not smart enough to know what's best for me, but here's what I'm asking You to do. After all, You invited me to bring my hassles to You."

● 3. **Their approach to Jesus was motivated by a keen awareness of His character.** If we closed this chapter without putting the spotlight on Jesus, we would miss the main thrust of Mark 5. *He* deserves top billing—not the demoniac nor Jairus nor the ailing woman.

Their knowledge of His *compassion* spurred them to drop their needs at His feet. Intuitively, they knew He would view their interruption as an opportunity rather than an annoyance. Though hundreds of spectators stalked His every step, they knew He'd show concern to one desperate individual vying for His attention.

God isn't "up there" somewhere—remote, impersonal, insensitive to individual needs. He isn't so busy managing the universe that He can't listen to your frustrations about school or your questions about the future. To the contrary, He cares enough to stop whatever else He's doing and listen. If you doubt that, just ask Jairus and the woman for a second opinion!

Love without strength, though, is nothing but weak sentimentality. Jesus' *power* also motivated Jairus and the woman to approach Him with their problems. They knew He was no ordinary man. Only someone of divine origin could restore a lame man, turn water into wine, calm a thunderstorm with a word, make demons cower in fear—all miracles that preceded their encounter with Him.

Think of it this way: Jesus' power gives His love an unlimited range of expression. I like the way Jeremiah put it: "Ah, Sovereign Lord, You have made the heavens and the earth by Your great power and outstretched arm. *Nothing is too hard for You*" (Jeremiah 32:17, italics added).

Let Jesus' compassion and power serve as the impetus to approach Him with your needs. Then approach Him with faith, boldness, and humility. But be prepared for an upheaval in the status quo. Just as the characters in Mark 5 were never the same, you too will experience transformation.

Learn from these Bible people, and watch God bring out the heroic potential in you.

MORE GREAT BOOKS FROM SONPOWER

Life-in-Focus
Filling Up Your Think Tank by Bill Stearns.
What's on your mind? This book will help you
explore your thoughts and start thinking the
way God wants you to. Find out how important
your mind really is. Textbook **6-2264**

Home Sweet Battleground? by Pamela Heim.
This book will help you learn how to commu-
nicate honestly with your parents. You'll understand them better and find out how to help
them see things your way too. Textbook
6-2586

Caution: Christians Under Construction by
Bill Hybels. Build your relationship with God
with the tools in this book. It will help you
work on your self-image, friendships, perseverance, and more. Textbook **6-2759**

Word-in-Focus

Faith Workout by Bill Myers. Exercise your faith and watch it grow stronger with this study of the Book of James. Stretch your faith in such areas as temptation, the tongue, and money. Textbook **6-2265**

New and Improved by James Long. You can have a better life—a better you—with God's help. This study of 1 John explores your tough questions about truth, love, doubt—living a better life God's way. Textbook **6-2590**

Follow the Leader by Dan Schmidt. Get on the road to discipleship with this study of the Book of Matthew. Find out what it was like to be one of Jesus' original 12 disciples, and what it means to follow Him today. Textbook **6-2629**

Leader's Guides with Multiuse Transparency Masters and Rip-Offs are available.